THE

FOOD&BEVERAGE
MAGAZINE

THE

FOOD&BEVERAGE
MAGAZINE

GUIDE TO

RESTAURANT
SUCCESS

The proven process for
starting any restaurant business
from scratch to success

MICHAEL POLITZ

WILEY

Published by John Wiley & Sons, Inc., Hoboken, New Jersey.
Published simultaneously in Canada.

For general information on our other products and services or for technical support, please contact our Customer Care Department within the United States at (800) 762-2974, outside the United States at (317) 572-3993 or fax (317) 572-4002.

Wiley publishes in a variety of print and electronic formats and by print-on-demand. Some material included with standard print versions of this book may not be included in e-books or in print-on-demand. If this book refers to media such as a CD or DVD that is not included in the version you purchased, you may download this material at http://booksupport.wiley.com. For more information about Wiley products, visit www.wiley.com.

Library of Congress Cataloging-in-Publication Data is Available:

ISBN 9781119668961 (Hardcover)
ISBN 9781119668954 (ePDF)
ISBN 9781119668985 (ePub)

Cover Design: Wiley
Cover Image: © A-Digit/Getty Images

Printed in the United States of America

V10018631_051820

This book is dedicated to my children, Shelby and Jett, with the loving support of Kaiulani, Julien, and Amora, who have never let me quit. By never quitting, I am always winning.

CONTENTS

INTRODUCTION: WHY YOU NEED THIS BOOK

So you want to open a restaurant, and you don't have millions of dollars to spend. This is your dream, your passion, and a goal you want to achieve, but you don't know where to start. Thousands of books can tell you how to start a business, succeed in the food and beverage industry, and achieve your aspirations and purpose. So what makes this one different? *The Food & Beverage Magazine Guide to Restaurant Success* is all of those books rolled into one.

This book will show you how to

- Determine if you are ready, willing, and able to open a restaurant
- Select the best location, menu, and staff
- Understand step-by-step how to open a restaurant
- Market your new restaurant
- Make smart decisions about where to invest your money to grow your business

"Experts" and naysayers will urge you not to open that business until you have millions of dollars to back you up. Clearly, you're not going to listen to them, because you're reading this book. Good for you.

The Most Important Thing to Remember

To begin, you *must* read this section over and over to understand this book.

If you are going to open and operate a successful restaurant, you *must* understand that it is a business, and you are now an entrepreneur. It doesn't matter if you are a mechanic, office worker, chef, sommelier, or foodie. Restaurateur is a nice label, but you *must* become an entrepreneur as well as use your other skills to open and then operate a successful restaurant.

Period.

What is an entrepreneur?

Do you watch popular television shows where people pitch business ideas, or successful entrepreneurs work with startups? While viewing these programs, do you yell at the screen or tell yourself you could do so much better? These shows are entertaining (or they wouldn't be on the air), but this is not what an entrepreneur does to become successful.

According to *Forbes* magazine, an entrepreneur is more than someone who owns and operates a business. That person is both a leader and a manager. As a leader, you find the solution to every problem, including hiring the right people to solve a particular issue. As a manager, you handle the day-to-day operations (until the situation changes). You understand the difference between finance and accounting. You recognize how marketing and sales are very different but that both are needed to be successful. You work long hours, get dirty, become frustrated, and would not live any differently. As an entrepreneur, you want autonomy, purpose, and flexibility, while making money and ultimately leaving a legacy. Most importantly, you are willing to pay the price in sacrifice, failure, and hard work with faith in yourself and what you want to accomplish.

My Start as an Entrepreneur

Usually, other "experts" would begin their book by telling you about their many successes in the food and beverage industry, hospitality industry, and business in general.

I am very successful, but more importantly, I want you to understand me as a person and entrepreneur. Using my guidance, you can open a restaurant without having millions of dollars to spend. I can open one today for as little as $25,000.

How? The steps will be explained throughout the book. For now, let's start at the beginning.

I was 8 years old, and I found a way to sell greeting and holiday cards. If I sold enough cards, I got points to pick a prize. Something inside of me said that I could move these cards by lugging boxes and selling them door-to-door. Making money this way, I would get to pick whatever prize I wanted.

I selected a shiny, new, brass-plated trumpet—and I have no idea why I picked that trumpet or what happened to it. My eye was on the prize, and while I remember the feeling of the importance of selling enough cards to select a reward, I can barely remember the prize itself.

As an entrepreneur, even at such a young age, that feeling kept me going. I realized that if I could sell those cards, I'd get that prize and much more. That was a defining moment that influences my life to this day.

However, my parents urged me to pursue a career as a professional. I do wonder where I would be today if I had become a lawyer or doctor. My dad (and everyone else) told me to do a lot of soul searching when I was trying to figure out what I wanted to do as a career. I was a little envious of others at the time; many people in my world already knew what they wanted to do and where their paths were going to take them.

I love and respect my family, especially my father, so I decided to attend college and obtain a degree. I had no plans or goals professionally; I was focused on getting an education. My personal plan was to attend college, learn everything I could, and hang out with my friends. What's more important than friends, fast cars, motorcycles, and good times?

Then a funny thing happened. I graduated from high school and planned to attend college, but I needed to make money, and I didn't want a job. Now I am going to show my age, but before the internet, there were classified advertisements in newspapers. They were like apps for buying and selling, except printed on paper. I always read the classifieds, especially businesses for sale. I can't explain why, but I loved reading that section daily. One day, I discovered an ad looking for people to rent an ice cream truck.

"Wow, that would be fun," I thought. "I can drive around all day." Gas prices at the time ranged from 89 cents to 99 cents per gallon. I wanted to do this, so I managed to get my best friend and cousin, Mark Mandel, involved (even though at the time he was not as inspired as I was by the idea and just wanted to sleep the summer away).

I had to go to an area that was not desirable to rent the truck, but I could keep the truck at my place. I was on my way.

Then I realized I had to buy the product wholesale to sell it retail. I called my friends and discovered that Alex Mates, my friend Paula Kaufman's boyfriend (now husband), operated a frozen foods business that supplied ice cream products to big grocery store chains. I knew I had to meet him.

I got my products from him wholesale, and I thought my ice cream truck was the greatest business ever. We loaded up the truck and used a loudspeaker to get people's attention by playing music. I even had friends who would breakdance on the roof. I offered raffles, so when you bought something, you got a raffle ticket. One of the prizes I offered was a doll from the movie *Gremlins*. Boxer Sugar Ray Leonard lived in one of the neighborhoods where I drove the ice cream truck, and his son Ray Jr. won the toy. Ray and I are still close friends, and he swears he doesn't remember any of this. We just laugh about it now.

That is the fun part of the story.

On the other hand, people would break into the truck and steal food and other items late at night. I soon realized that it was my responsibility if the truck broke down, I didn't get the right product, or people didn't feel like working that day. At the end of the summer, we had made enough to cover our product costs and pay for gas.

I loved it. I learned about commerce, people, food, licensing, and being my own boss. Since that experience gave me access to other frozen food products at wholesale prices, I offered other products to customers for retail prices. Operating this business taught me a lot about that aspect of the food and beverage industry.

Then I attended the University of Maryland as a hotshot freshman at the age of 18, and somehow I ended up in the t-shirt business. I sold t-shirts across the campus from a backpack. Once I transferred to the American University Kogod School of Business in Washington, D.C., I started a flower business. I sold roses for $9.99, walking around with the same backpack, this time full of flyers that I stapled to the bulletin boards around school, and made sales. I even enlisted two of my fraternity brothers, Eric Simkin and Lee Perlman, to help facilitate sales in the business.

I knew then that I was going to become an entrepreneur. I planned to build vast wealth on my own by selling products, coming up with ideas, and creating and developing new ways to earn money. I didn't know the specifics yet. I just knew that I didn't want to become a lawyer or doctor when I could be an entrepreneur instead.

I went to school, graduated, and got my bachelor of science degree in business administration from the Kogod School of Business at American University.

Once I moved on from the floral industry, I realized that I understood the concept of marketing for the restaurant and hospitality industries. I decided at that point to publish a magazine for the food and beverage industry. It was the perfect target audience for a target advertiser such as myself.

Fast-forward to 30 years later.

I consulted with many people about opening restaurants. But after reading and learning about the successes (and failures) of many restaurants in my magazine, blogs, and marketing and consulting businesses, I wanted to delve into owning and operating a restaurant.

Growing up back east, my dad had a friend, Chuck Rossler, who owned and operated a restaurant called Celebrity Deli. Chuck was the greatest guy ever. We would go to this small hole-in-the-wall in a strip center, and Chuck was bigger than life. His kids, Julie and Jon, and I were friends, and I loved going there. After my teenage years, it became my place to meet people to expand my flower business. I witnessed Chuck hustling and moving all the time. There were lines out the door, and I saw Chuck as a rock star. He was one of the many restaurateurs I observed celebrating the joy of owning a restaurant, regardless of its size or scope.

Almost 25 years later, in 2012, I decided to invest $25,000 to open a fast food–style restaurant that was not part of a franchise. I knew I needed to find a second-generation restaurant with equipment. I also needed to select a restaurant that would fulfill a need in a specific community or neighborhood.

I chose a restaurant located in a gas station in the north part of Las Vegas. I developed the concept of specialty mini burgers that were not offered anywhere else in the valley. My idea came from Little Tavern in Washington, D.C., which made burgers using little balls of meat with onions; the mini burgers were flattened with a spatula, grilled, put on a small bun, and placed in a steaming machine. My friends and I loved this place and its food, and I wanted to re-create it.

I had the concept, found the location, and got my licenses. I paid $3,500 a month in rent, which included everything. However, the location in the gas station was not conducive to capturing every customer coming into the business. While there were lines out the door, the neighborhood was considered sketchy, and I realized selecting that location was not my best decision. I decided to move the restaurant and started another one with the same budget of $25,000.

I am a great marketer, and I can get people in the door. However, I discovered that I was not as knowledgeable about back-of-house operations and keeping up with demand. I also selected the wrong partner to help with that aspect, and his philosophy was different from mine.

I eventually got it right and opened four more locations offering burgers (with or without cheese), fries, chicken sandwiches, chili, birthday cake (everyone loves a birthday cake), and milkshakes (vanilla or chocolate syrup poured in, but not stirred). My chili was called 239 Bean Chili: when someone asked about the number, the answer was that adding one more bean would make it too farty. That was an old joke my dad used to tell us—it was a great marketing tool and added to the chili's success on the menu.

Soon after, I decided to sell the business.

I owned and operated many businesses in the food and beverage industry. Some were more successful than others. I sold some and closed others. When you are an entrepreneur, you are willing to give up your current businesses to pursue new challenges. I always like to live like a creek: when the water hits a rock, it jumps in another direction instead of pooling and becoming stagnant.

Restaurateur as Entrepreneur

Entrepreneurs jump into any business that tickles them, reaches their core, and becomes more than another goal. Most of the time, there's not a lot of soul searching needed. Entrepreneurs just know. They have decided what to do, how they want to do it, and where they want to go.

The problem is, they don't know what paths to take. They know where they want to be as well as the outcome. I think that's what happens when people jump into any business, especially the food and beverage industry.

You have a fantastic family recipe for your grandma's pasta sauce or great carrot cake or a trend-setting gin cocktail. Should you find a manufacturer and distributor to package and sell that sauce? What about topping off some pasta with that sauce in a restaurant? Should you open a bakery?

You want to share this culinary delight with the world and make money doing it. How do you make that happen? You need to be both a restaurateur and an entrepreneur.

I will guide you, help you learn the steps, and figure out how you can make that restaurant, bakery, food truck, or other food establishment become a reality. You are going to learn from my and everybody else's failures. Over the decades of owning, operating, and publishing *Food & Beverage Magazine*, I have witnessed it all. I've seen thousands of failures and hundreds of successes.

I believe we can learn more from the failures than the successes. Yes, many successful businesses started with a huge bankroll or big celebrity name. But that's not necessarily the secret ingredient for success or the cure for failure.

You do need to do some soul searching about what *you* want. Is it a career, a second career, the opportunity to be your own boss, or a side job? Do you want to do this for the love of food or the love of money? Do you want to build something for your future or your children's future? What's the reason? Do you love to serve people? Do you want to clean their dirty dishes? What is your ideal end result?

Reality Check for Your Dreams

Reading this book, you might be saying, "Yes, I *want* to own a restaurant."

Let me tell you the fantasy that many people have when they say that. In this vision, you show up when you want to (after all, you are the boss). You go from table to table, talking to the customers, or sit at the bar and socialize. You have a dedicated staff that takes care of every detail. You can account for all of your revenue. You constantly vacation because your presence is not required, and you make a lot of money. Your restaurant is a well-oiled machine that can operate almost on its own.

Nice dream.

In my own experience, the glamour dissipates very fast after opening a restaurant, especially if you're working with friends. If there are no customers, your money dissolves even faster. You are on call 24/7 (regardless of the hours the business is open), you clean bathrooms, you take out the garbage, and you cover shifts while cash and products "walk" out of the door.

You need to think about finding your way through life's questions. What is it that I want to do? How am I going to do this? Am I willing to put in the work? Am I willing to fail? Am I willing to take that risk, fail, and realize what failure means? Most importantly, what does failure mean to me?

Everyone's failure is different. Sometimes it can be financial; sometimes it is an attack on your character. That's something only you know. Personally, my failure is not always monetary. I like longevity. That is why I consider the *Food & Beverage Magazine* a success after being in business for over 20 years.

The magazine has had its ups and downs financially. One of the things I am going to talk about throughout the book is riding out these ups and downs. Life is a roller coaster, and if you don't get enough momentum going down, you'll never get up that next hill. So slamming on the brakes on the way down will not help you whatsoever. That is one lesson you will learn quickly.

These are some of the many things an entrepreneur (restaurateur) needs to consider. I have a passion for being of service to people in the hospitality industry. Hearing success stories growing up, all I ever wanted to do was read *Entrepreneur* or *Inc.* magazine about how to become successful. I wanted to be one of those guys. When I was 27, I finally had my chance, and I was listed in *Entrepreneur* magazine as one of the top 40 entrepreneurs under 40 years old in the country. While that was a highlight of my career, I was going to make sure it was not the only highlight of my life.

Can you be of service to your staff, suppliers, and customers as well as yourself? Being an entrepreneur comes with its own set of rules and values. Entrepreneurs like Richard Branson and Mark Cuban have fans and people who want to live just like them. It is not about fame and fortune (although financial success is terrific). It is about admiration and the desire to craft your life just like theirs as an entrepreneur (restaurateur). When you were a little kid, did you want to go to McDonald's to meet Ronald McDonald because you thought he owned it? That is the spirit of an entrepreneur.

If you are ready, let's continue. I look forward to eating and drinking at your new establishment soon.

1 Recipe for Success

I can feel your excitement through these pages as you begin to read, anxious to open that restaurant. You are ready for the next steps—picking a location, deciding on the menu, and preparing to jump feet first into this great adventure. The very first step is . . . searching your soul, brainstorming, and really delving into your psyche to determine if you really want to open a restaurant and be in the hospitality industry.

I will take you step-by-step through the process to determine if you should pursue this venture. I have met people who were born to be in the food and beverage industry. Others tried and realized this is not their path to happiness.

I have friends who tell me that they just want to prepare meat by smoking it all day. They tell me how they love brining it and cooking it; to them, this is art. They delight in making the perfect burnt ends and unbelievable bark. Others want to create vegan options like carrots that taste like hotdogs. That is their passion. I know others with the same inspiration, drive, and single-minded purpose when it comes to food and beverage.

Together, let's discover if you are one of those people who yearn to be of service to others and should open a restaurant, or someone who should go in a different direction.

Soul Searching: Is Food and Beverage Part of Your DNA?

You are on your career path, and there is a yearning desire that won't go away. You feel that you are not following your destiny: something is missing, and you don't just *want* to open a restaurant, you *have to*, or your soul will wither and die.

Or on a more practical level, do you see owning a restaurant to

- Make money?
- Become famous? or
- Overcome a challenge?

My suggestion is to write down your answers, either on a legal yellow pad or on a whiteboard. On the left side, start with your pros; and on the right side, list your cons. It is this simple. Your pros and cons will become clear as you begin to write down the answers to the questions. Here are some other questions you need to ask and answer before you go any further with this business:

Do you love the food and beverage industry?

Are you willing to take a risk with your money?

Do you have family and friends willing to take a risk with their money?

Do you have the necessary relationships, or are you willing to cultivate them, including vendors, staff, media, and other people in the food and beverage industry?

Along with relationships with others in the industry, are you willing to create relationships with your customers?

Do you have the time and patience to research all aspects of opening a restaurant, such as food supply, real estate, hiring staff, licensing, marketing, and the competition, just to name a few of the areas? This book will help you with those details of what, where, and how to research. One of the most-used words in this book is *research*, and many areas need research for success in order for your restaurant to succeed. So, are you ready to start spending quiet time in front of a computer and doing your research?

What is your competitive advantage?

- Is your family in the restaurant business?
- Do you have a restaurant background?
- Are you in possession of award-winning recipes?
- Are you trained as a chef?
- Are you trained as a sommelier?
- Do you own the real estate (building, land, space)?

Does the community where the restaurant will be located need and/or desire this establishment or the cuisine? What are the demographics?

Can you handle the competition? Can the competition handle you?

What makes you different and/or better?

Can you leave your ego at the door—knowing you will work 10 times as hard with all of the responsibility?

Can you handle adverse reactions when you drop the bomb that you want to open a business with a 60% chance of failure in the first three years? How will you feel when your family and friends *don't* support your decision?

Next, reading the following statements, what fits with your concept of opening a restaurant?

- My place will feature great recipes, especially from my family.
- My place will become a great place for friends to hang out.
- I love food.
- I have this artful expression of skills.
- It's sexy.

- I can do it better than others.
- I can become wealthy.
- I am passionate about other restaurants and the industry as a whole.
- I am ready to conquer uncharted territory, become a pioneer, and make my mark on the industry.

How will you handle angry customers, vendors, staff, and food critics?

How do you define success?

What are your motivations?

Can you handle aggressive salespeople? Are you able to tell the difference between a new trend and a sales pitch?

Do you give in to salespeople, staff, or customers under pressure? How do you handle confrontation (which is not necessarily combative or negative)?

What are you going to do when times are rough? How will you handle missed deliveries, absent staff, price increases for ingredients, taxes, lack of customers, bad advertising decisions, bad reviews, and other challenges while making no money?

What are your expectations and long-term goals?

Like an Onion: Cut Through the Layers

You need to really examine yourself.

While devices and notebooks are great, this is where you need to use your yellow legal pad and find your favorite pen or pencil. Then write down the following statements:

- I am a motivated person.
- I am a self-starter.

- I am a great problem solver.
- I handle stress well.
- I am an organized person.
- I manage my time well.
- I handle rejection well.
- I handle criticism well.
- I am a good sport.
- I handle success well.
- I am responsible with money.
- I am a people person.
- I love to mop floors, wipe tables, and clean dishes.
- I love to scrub a grill and clean dirty oil from a fryer.

Rate yourself on a scale from 1 to 10 for each statement, and see where your personality and temperament fall on the scale. Then, select people you trust and see if they agree with your assessment of yourself.

Facing the Critics, Doubters, and Naysayers

When you share your dream of actually opening a restaurant, do your friends and family tell you that you must be insane? You know these are the same people in your life who told you that your food is fantastic and you should open a restaurant. What will you say when people ask why you invested in a business with a high failure rate? According to CNBC, 60% of new restaurants fail within the first year as of 2016. But according to Upserve Restaurant Insider, projected sales for restaurants in 2018 were $825 billion, with Americans spending 48% of their total food budget to dine out. Don't let those figures give you the wrong impression. Industry growth is no guarantee you will succeed.

How do you differentiate from those who are scared about your decision because of what they heard about the industry and those who tell you not to open a restaurant because they don't understand you and the entrepreneurial life you choose?

Also, what impact will opening a restaurant have on your family? Most people can't work a full-time job and operate a restaurant. That means they need to quit their job and focus on the restaurant. There is financing that could involve taking out a loan or second mortgage. How will this impact your immediate family? They certainly have a different perspective than your parents, siblings, aunts, uncles, cousins, and other family members. Your friends will view your decisions differently, and either you thank them for their concern or ask them for help.

Only You Can Make Your Dreams Come True

You love to invite people over for Sunday dinner. You make the best meals (whatever they may be), and everyone who comes over tells you that you should open a restaurant. You may be bombarded with a million thoughts of insecurity, or it may simply reinforce what you already know about your desire to open a restaurant. A channel is opened, and you ask yourself, "Why aren't you pursuing this dream?" Then self-doubt raises its ugly head, and you give yourself many excuses why this dream can't happen.

Fear grips you. However, dreams are not built on fear or excuses. The truth is, most of the believed obstacles are not real and not part of reality. I once heard that fear and anxiety are when someone worries about the future instead of focusing on the right now. Some people will back down, wonder "what if," and stick to a safe career path.

I was raised that "can't is not an option" and obstacles are challenges. This is part of the soul-searching process. Are you able to overcome these challenges? I have discovered that entrepreneurs thrive on challenges. They embrace them. Entrepreneurs tell the world to watch them as they show how they can do this and accomplish that. Just the thought that it can be done leads the entrepreneur down the path of doing it. This was my path to entering the food and beverage industry as a part of the broader hospitality industry.

What about you? Are you able to get past the fear of the future and self-doubt and move forward, actually becoming excited about this new adventure?

Opening a Restaurant Makes Me Warm and Fuzzy

There was a time I was pitching a television show about food called *Family Traditions*. My friend, actor Louis Lombardi, and I wanted to travel around the country and interview people who cook family recipes that create traditions. I have discovered that this is probably the number-one reason people open a restaurant. They tell you about their grandmother's gravy recipe (don't call it *sauce* in some Italian households). People go into detail about growing the tomatoes, and the proper way of preserving the tomatoes, until then *and only then* are the tomatoes ready to combine with the other ingredients. Other people remember the times they went to the ballpark with their dad and shared hot dogs, so now they want to open a restaurant selling hot dogs.

One of my closest friends and mentors, the late, great Chef Kerry Simon, created dishes that would genuinely touch your heart. He took snack cakes, cotton candy, and other comfort foods such as meatloaf and made them his own. People enjoyed them, and it brought back their own memories. This is a feeling that is hard to convey. Even chains are now trying to create a family atmosphere, but it is a contrived, Hollywood set; most people search out chef-owned, family-owned, or individually owned places to dine.

Caveat—just because you have terrific memories tied to food doesn't mean you can open a restaurant. This is part of your soul searching. You have great stories to go with the food, and you can share them with the public. Still, this does not mean people will line up to try that food.

The One Ingredient to Use Sparingly—Ego

You need confidence, belief in yourself, and, yes, a healthy ego telling you that you are talented, are creative, and can accomplish this dream.

What you don't need is such a big ego that you believe you are too good to wash dishes, treat your staff with respect, or accept other people's constructive criticism. In fact, you should never wonder how people could *dare* to criticize you, your food, or your restaurant. Yes, there will be haters and those who are jealous of your drive and ambition to make your dream a reality. However, some people with experience and expertise want you to succeed and are willing to share their opinion and advice.

Here is the scenario. You have a fantastic recipe. Your family loves it, your friends rave about it, and everyone you know who has tried the recipe enthusiastically endorses you and the dish. You are inspired to open a restaurant, just *knowing* everybody will eat there just for that dish on the menu.

You are on top of the world with a full wind in your sails, so to speak, and you are ready to conqueror the food and beverage industry. You envision yourself on top of a mountain; arms spread wide as you survey the landscape below, *knowing* your dish and restaurant will become the talk of the town, and you are the greatest!

Then something horrible happens!

Customers actually don't like the recipe and won't return to your restaurant. A vendor might start to criticize the recipe (or its ingredients) and tell you they have better options. One of the ingredients is not available, or there is a spike in its price. A trend overtakes the culinary landscape, and your main ingredient is "bad" or unhealthy or, worse, old school. Then comes the dreaded review that blasts you, your dish, your restaurant, and the fact that you are still open for business.

If you have a big ego, you can be crushed as you see yourself tumbling down the mountain into a crumpled pile of despair.

But if you see this as a bump in the road, you can ride out the storm.

Customers will complain to the manager, post how much they hate the restaurant on social media, and then write a bad review. How are you going to handle that? Will a big ego get in the way, or are you going to handle this situation using a fair, reasonable, and logical approach?

You can't take anything personally, because it's not personal. It's the customer's acquired taste, and you have to be prepared for that. Some people will never be satisfied. It is the nature of the business. Food and beverage is very personal. If you take any of this personally and become belligerent, ego-driven, and put your walls up, you will probably never succeed in the hospitality industry.

Recently, a friend told me that I must try the greatest chocolate chip cookie that I would ever eat. I explained patiently that I hear this about food every day, and I refused to try the cookie. Well, he was persistent, so I decided that I needed to eat one of these cookies and see if I agreed with my friend. The baker told me that only one person of the many who had tried his cookies did not like them.

I ate the cookie.

It was the greatest cookie I ever tasted, literally.

I decided to call another friend who owns and operates one of the largest vending companies in the country. I knew that if he liked this cookie, we could package it and sell it through his vending infrastructure. This was a home run—my latest million-dollar idea. I was about to be the cookie king of the world!

I was told by the baker that there was no way this vending machine company owner would not like the cookie, since everybody so far who had tasted the cookie had loved it.

The owner of the vending machine company was visiting Las Vegas, so I had a basket of the freshly baked cookies delivered directly to his plane when he landed.

He tasted the cookie.

He didn't like it. He told me that he thought the outside of the cookie tasted stale even though it was a fresh batch. Just like that, I wasn't the cookie king anymore.

Now I had to tell this to the baker. I wondered before I told him if he was equipped to handle the truth, reminding me of the film, *A Few Good Men*, when Jack Nicholson's character screams, "You can't handle the truth."

The baker had bragged about only one person not liking his cookies, but now there were two, and the second one could have created more business (and success) for him. How did the baker handle this criticism?

It was awful. I will leave it at that, since he is not a client of mine, but even though I think his cookies are the greatest cookies I have ever tasted, I predict he won't go far. His ego is getting in the way of either fixing something or persevering without taking it personally.

I would have advised him not to consider this a failure but rather just one of the many bumps when you are part of the food and beverage industry. Yes, this was a big one, since the baker could conceivably have made millions if the vending machine company owner had loved his cookies.

The baker can fix the problem if he believes the input. If the baker believes in his recipe and someone doesn't like it, he is okay with keeping the recipe. A good restaurateur will really examine the other person's opinion calmly, decide on a course of action, and stick with it.

If anyone gets defensive, makes excuses, and becomes confrontational in the restaurant industry, they will probably go out of business.

But My Mom Likes My Recipe

What about your friends and family? You know, the people in your life who told you that your food is fantastic. How would you feel if they criticized something and gave suggestions on how to fix it?

Here is a harsh reality. I am not just being negative—I want you to succeed. But many people are expecting you to fail and will go after you because no one really wants you to succeed except maybe your mom and dad. Don't rely on your family and friends to be your steady customers because they won't show up, and if they do, they may expect free food. You need to realize that haters are going to hate. Friends and family (other than your mother and father) become jealous of you following those dreams to make them a reality. Many people want their own dreams to succeed, and when they see someone else accomplishing their goals, they get triggered. Many people just don't have the mental capacity to be unselfishly happy for someone else.

You need to entice people to try your new place instead of sticking with something familiar. It can be a hard sell, but it can be done with your personality and positive attitude. This includes receiving any criticism, bad review, or complaint and handling all of them positively and favorably for everyone involved.

However, once you get them through your front door, people will come to the restaurant with a positive attitude. They are spending their time and money and want a great experience. As for social media and other review sites, people who post regularly enter a restaurant with a little more awareness of mistakes and problems. If a mistake or problem is pointed out, that means something needs to be fixed, and I see this as a positive.

I kept my ego out of my business and understood the difference between constructive criticism and negativity. I hate criticism like most people, but I can determine whether it is something that should be changed or just someone hating. I realize people can be negative by nature. If you give everything you can for the best possible dining experience, people can't complain. They can criticize, but not complain. You need to know the difference, and you have to view this as a challenge and not a personal attack. Simply be of service to everyone and hold true to your mission. Hedge your bets, mitigate any problems, and you will have a customer for life, including family and friends.

How Do I Become a Great Chef or Restaurateur Above the Others?

If becoming a great chef or restaurateur so you can look down on people is your goal, then this book is not for you.

Yes, there are movies such as *Ratatouille*, *Chef*, and *No Reservations* about chefs. There are great TV shows with the late Anthony Bourdain and Andrew Zimmern. But what draws audiences is that there are no big egos involved. The chefs are willing to try anything even though they might not know how to cook it.

The stereotype of the egotistical French chefs is gone. That barrier has been totally broken with new chefs of the twenty-first century. However, I believe media still portrays great chefs with a big ego, and, yes, I have known chefs with huge egos. But in the end, the chefs would joke about themselves because they realized as they got older that they didn't need to be pompous and that they made mistakes like everyone else.

Chefs and restaurateurs must be confident in what they do but not arrogant or egotistical. Restaurateurs who own nationally acclaimed restaurants, including Wolfgang Puck, Piero Selvaggio,

Nobuyuki "Nobu" Matsuhisa, and the late chef Paul Prudhomme, were among the most humble restaurateurs and supporters of me when I first started, and I am honored that I can now be their voice to you.

I Need a Shoulder to Cry On

Are you able to handle everything without complaining to everyone or, worse, posting on social media?

Don't whine to your family and friends. They will perceive (right or wrong) that you made a huge mistake and need to walk away *now*. This would be putting your restaurant in an awful light.

Yes, find one or two confidants or a mentor in the industry (not a vendor, please) you can vent, talk, complain, and whine to, and just get it out of your system. For everyone else, including mom and dad, keep the smile on your face and only talk in positives when it comes to the restaurant. While I am not a psychologist, negative talk colors a person's experience, and you want everyone to have the most positive, pleasant, and memorable experience possible at your restaurant.

Show Me the Money

When considering opening a restaurant, you need to determine how much you personally have to invest and how much money you will need to make your dream a reality.

This is financing.

Let me explain—financing is not just obtaining a loan. It is spending money to open a business, regardless of the source of the funds. That includes using savings, cashing out your 401k, taking out a second mortgage (which I don't advise), and obtaining loans from a financial institution, investors, or family and friends.

How much do you need to get started?

This depends on the type of restaurant you want to open, the space you will lease or own, and whether the space has already been built out as a restaurant and what equipment is included.

Living in Las Vegas, many people approach me about opening a restaurant and investing $3 to $5 million. What they don't understand is that it is almost impossible to make back that much money owning a restaurant. I have seen many people invest that much money and lose it.

As for raising the funding, the book will explore the options, but right now you need to determine the amount of money you can raise and invest before you go any further in deciding to open a restaurant.

If you decide you want to open a restaurant and you have at least $25,000, this book can help you open that restaurant. If you have $100,000 or more, this book will be just as valuable. If your restaurant is successful, you will make back your original investment.

Throughout the book, I will advise you on sourcing, equipment, and even finding a restaurant that will be ready to open almost immediately after some modifications. If you want to open a steakhouse on limited financing (not the budget), you can find a restaurant that has been closed but will include the equipment as well as space. The same is true for restaurants that feature burgers, pizza, and other cuisines, which could save you over $50,000. If you are financing your restaurant for $25,000, and you find the perfect space, there is money you are not spending on the location that you can use in other areas.

There are third-, fourth-, and fifth-generation restaurant spaces that offer even more equipment that will save you money. However, it may cost you to have the equipment serviced and cleaned. Most of the equipment is made of metal and can be cleaned, and I have spent a lot of money to have old fryers scrubbed to the point that they shine. Sometime you will have to replace a temperature gauge or heating filament. The worst-case scenario I have found is when you have to replace the compressor, which is expensive. However, sometimes the landlord will repair and replace the equipment to lease the place, so definitely ask them. You won't have new, state-of-the-art technology, but you don't need that right now. If you can save over $100,000 by renting an older restaurant space with the necessary equipment including tables and chairs, go for it! This will enable you to have more options in opening a restaurant.

It can be done if you follow this book and, more importantly, really want to open a restaurant.

Money Is Great, but the Value of Other Things Is Bigger and Better

Entrepreneurs list their assets other than financial. One of the most valuable assets anyone can have is a relationship. When I was 18, it was through a friend that I met a person running a wholesale frozen food business to supply my ice cream truck that I wrote about in the introduction. He taught me a lot when I was operating that ice cream truck as a teenager. I credit much of my entrepreneurial success to my relationships.

You need to write a list of everyone you know—professionally, personally, or on social media. Then you need to develop a list of people to establish relationships, including vendors and others in the industry. This is not meant to be viewed as using people or seeing what you can get out of knowing someone. However, you need to know what they can do to help you as well as what you can do to help them (without going broke by offering 50 of their closest friends free food). Don't be unreasonable and expect everything from them; but people do love to help, and this is very valuable for success.

When I started the magazine, I put together an advisory board, including chefs Wolfgang Puck, Bobby Flay, Kerry Simon, and others. Wolfgang gave me his vendor list and told me to use his name when I called them. Bobby said to me that he wanted to help me build up the magazine. I was able to develop this advisory board because I met these people and developed relationships. But most important to my success was the friendship I had with television personality Robin Leach, famous for hosting *Lifestyles of the Rich and Famous*. Robin taught me the value of these relationships and how to intertwine them into my success. He emphasized always giving more than receiving and learning from the successes and the failures of high-profile people. He taught me that we never stop learning and should always be building new relationships.

If you already have family and friends in the food and beverage industry, that is great. Do you know any celebrities, including entertainment and sports figures? Do friends of friends know any personalities? While maybe A-listers would not be interested, it is a celebrity-driven society, and people want to meet celebs even if the personalities' peak was 20 years ago. People also love to read about personalities eating at a restaurant. If you cultivate a professional (or personal) relationship with celebrities, and do not ask for an investment, you can get that extra push.

There are foodie influencers on Facebook and Instagram who can get the word out. The fascinating aspect of social media is that influencers are more accessible, and I would recommend that you cultivate relationships with them.

Are you ready, willing, and able to do that?

Can You Change With the Times?

I began a business selling roses for $9.99 per dozen, eventually adding the wholesale component and transforming the business as part of a mega-million dollar industry. Then the industry changed, with supermarkets and other big-box retailers offering flowers at discounted prices. I then changed directions and went into the publishing industry.

Business models change, and as an entrepreneur, I needed to accept change to continue my success. I asked myself, "What is it that I love?" I loved hospitality, especially the food and beverage industry, and the fact that there was a targeted audience. I decided to enter it as a publisher of a magazine and be a voice in the industry.

Are you able to think like an entrepreneur in an ever-changing market in order to succeed? You've got to be able to move at the speed of light in a different direction. You can't become too attached to the food, or a venue, or a theme. Restaurants that were staples in the American landscape have closed or are losing money. McDonald's, one of the most successful restaurants of all time, customizes its menu by location (domestically and internationally). Two of the biggest trends as of publication are avocado toast and boneless chicken wings. I didn't know wings could be made without bones. Delivery technology and plant-based dishes are shaking up the hospitality industry. Franchises' and chains' profits are plummeting, and I believe it is because the price point is too high and the quality has diminished. Can you learn from their mistakes as well as follow a trend if it fits your restaurant?

Yes, there are favorites, but a real entrepreneur can determine when favorites remain profitable and not ego-driven. Are you motivated that way? Can you let something go, leave it behind, and start something new?

Are You Ready to Begin?

Most importantly, after considering all of your answers to the questions in this chapter, can you still say you love this industry and want to serve people and become successful? If you said yes (and meant it), your personal foundation has been set, and now it is time to begin working on and learning about starting a restaurant.

2 Taking Those First Steps

You have searched your soul, talked to your family and friends, and read and reread the previous chapter, and you are ready to take that first step into owning a restaurant.

Congratulations—how are you feeling?

You should be feeling excited, anxious to get started, and thrilled that you are following your dream. If not, reread Chapter 1.

If you just can't wait to get started (and have even skimmed through the whole book), you will read this word frequently throughout the chapter: *research*.

Before you commit to a cuisine, location, and scheduled opening date, you will research, research, and research. Are you prepared? Are you ready to study? Are you willing to make decisions? Let's open your restaurant.

Buy a package of yellow pads or notebooks to write notes. Yes, you can work digitally, but written notes will be needed as well.

Cuisine: What Do You Want to Feed Your Customers?

You probably have an idea of what you want to feature in your restaurant.

Remember the fantastic recipe that all your friends said is terrific, which is why you're going into the restaurant business.

When I owned and operated my hamburger places, my chili ingredients included cola and cinnamon. People would come for the little mini burgers, but they would lose their minds over the chili because they had never tasted a flavor like that. It was a standout. I added the marketing line that it was a 239-bean chili because if one more bean were added, it would be too farty. Between the flavor and the humorous tag line, my chili was a hit—and that meant profit.

Using chili as an example, you need to build what it takes to make your chili, so break down your recipe. Will you offer a vegan chili? Will it be meat and beans, or meatless? What kind of cheese will you use? Will you shred it yourself or buy it already shredded? What kind of beans will you use? What type of meat? What other ingredients do you need? What spices will you use? You need to break down this one dish into precise details.

Let's talk about fries, which could be a staple of a restaurant featuring chili. They could be French fries, waffle-cut steak fries, skinny fries, shoestring fries, or sweet potato fries. How are you going to salt them—sugar salt or just salt, and what kind of salt? At my restaurants, I tossed the fries directly from the fryer with a seasoning combining sugar, salt, and vinegar powder. Customers would come in and, after trying our fries, would rave about the chili and fries.

What else will you offer on the menu? What about hot dogs, hamburgers, and nachos? You might say that the focus of this restaurant is chili. But the chili was simply a side dish to the burgers. What other items can you offer to make it a complete menu for your concept? Can you use the same ingredients, like the cheese or the meat, in a variety of menu items?

Look at all your recipes and list the ingredients just like you did for the chili and fries. What else could you make with those ingredients? I advise you to minimize the list and see what recipes use the same ingredients. That will keep your costs down and help to ensure that you never run out of inventory.

You need standouts on your menu. While you might offer other dishes, you need one or two items that bring the customers back. For example, Ben's Chili Bowl (benschilibowl.com) in Washington, D.C., brings in presidents and other dignitaries. Check out the menu and see what keeps bringing people back to eat there.

A lesson I learned from the menu developers of a well-known chain is that their menu looks enormous, with many selections. If you break down the menu by ingredients, most of the items use the same ingredients, and it is a very short list. The menu offers dishes that can mix and match everything, and the restaurant offers a big menu to capture and target its audience.

This is the beginning of working on your business using a menu as your tool, but this is not your final menu. You are in the process of compiling data and information, and deciding on the food and drink you want to sell and other menu items that complement your featured items. You're going to change all this later, but you need to start now.

Using the example of steak, let's say you love preparing and cooking meat, and your first choice is opening a steak house. You're finding that it is out of your budget to open the restaurant as a steak house. You don't have to change the menu, just the presentation, such as a fast-casual place serving steak. Another option is subleasing a kitchen in a local pub or bar. The current owners may not want to run the restaurant portion, but they may be required to offer a certain percentage of food to alcohol sold ratio. This is another way to start a restaurant business.

When it comes to alcoholic beverages, will you serve wine; wine and beer; or wine, beer, and spirits? That's going to determine your location, which is then the next step. You will also need a liquor license.

So whether it is a chili place, a steak house, or a restaurant offering burgers, pasta, or plant-based foods, you need to decide on the cuisine and what you want to offer. The key is the menu creation, because if you don't have a menu, you don't have a restaurant.

What Do You Need Before Looking for the Right Location?

Determining the menu is the first step because the next question is, what do you need in your restaurant?

You first need to list the equipment—but don't research the cost yet. Just have a list of the equipment required.

On your list, you better have a three-compartment sink and grease trap and grill hood, because without the three-compartment sink, the restaurant won't be issued an important health license. Without a grease trap and hood, you can't fry or grill anything. It is all about options.

A lot of older restaurants don't have a grease trap, and that may be why they are on the market. If you have to put in a grease trap, it will cost thousands of dollars. There are portable grease traps on the market, but in most municipalities, they don't meet compliance.

Those are the first two things to look for in a possible location. You can contact your local health department and find out what other equipment is required to pass an inspection and get your health certificate. Be aware that walls and floors also have to be compliant, especially in the kitchen. More about the health department and compliance will be discussed in the next chapter.

You'll need other equipment such as refrigeration, ovens, freezers, and appliances such as mixers, food processors, and blenders. There are many websites that list restaurant equipment checklists. Type "What equipment do I need to open a restaurant?" in your search tab, and over 150,000 links will appear. You can create your list from these resources.

You can now begin to cost out equipment based on the type of restaurant you want to open. Research eCommerce sites and other sources, and then list just the initial costs for the equipment you must have to open a restaurant. After compiling your detailed list, you can start searching online restaurant equipment auction sites such as RestaurantEquipment.bid and classified sites including Facebook marketplaces and Craigslist as well as the classifieds in the local newspaper. You will eventually find the most cost-effective, used equipment.

Just Because It Is Open Doesn't Mean Customers Will Come

We have all heard the saying—location, location, location. This is the very first thing people have told me as an entrepreneur all my life. I don't believe it. If you've got something good, I believe people will travel to you. However, there are still many considerations to research and understand when choosing a location.

Let me explain using three examples.

Food Court

You are offered a key location in the food court in a busy shopping mall. This is not necessarily a winning location. You are competing with national brands and franchises. If your concept competes with them, you might not be allowed to offer that item under your contract; or worse, you might have to compete with them. You also need to consider that the landscape of malls in America is changing. Gone are the days when people just hung out at a mall and wanted to eat in a fast-casual environment. Malls are being transformed into places offering attractions, museums, and art galleries with a totally different demographic, and they include different casual and high-end restaurants.

Do Snowbirds Eat Ice Cream in the Winter?

Mesquite, Nevada, is 80 miles northeast of Las Vegas, and in the summertime the average temperatures are above 110 degrees with evening temperatures hovering around 80 degrees. A nationally well-known ice cream franchise opened a store there with its franchisees probably expecting a windfall and that they would make more money than they could spend.

However, they didn't do their research.

Mesquite is a snowbird community, meaning many residents leave around April and don't return until September. According to AreaVibes.com, the median age is 55, and only 28% of the population has children under the age of 18. The store, located in a free-standing strip mall, eventually closed.

This is not to say that the residents of Mesquite don't like ice cream. But half the population is gone during the summer months, and there was not enough business to sustain the store during the winter months. However, Mesquite is a gaming town with casinos. There is a small airport outside of Mesquite, but the majority of tourists drive into town, either in their own vehicles or on bus tours. This would have been a time that I would have recommended opening an ice cream shop either in one of the casinos or close to the casinos in a gas station, to capture tourists along with the locals.

Fresh Fish in the High Desert

Mesquite is 42 miles southwest of St. George, Utah, where there is a very successful restaurant, Hawaiian Poke Bowl. In fact, it is my favorite poke restaurant in the country. It is sold out of poke every day by 2 p.m. and has to close until the next day.

This restaurant became part of the big trend in poke bowl-type restaurants across the country. My friend, actor and comedian Jon Lovitz, was the first person to tell me about this trend. He traveled to various places in the country for different movie roles and saw these restaurants popping up everywhere.

For those of you who have never tried poke, the word *poke* is Hawaiian for "to slice or cut crosswise into pieces." *Poke* or *poke bowl* is diced raw fish served with rice. The fish used include yellowfin tuna, salmon, and shellfish seasoned with salt, soy sauce, sesame oil, and chili pepper.

But in the middle of the southern Utah desert, a successful poke restaurant is an unexplainable phenomenon. I was introduced to this amazing place by one of my family members, Shelley Fitzsimmons Turner, and Ben Schouten. Consider that an ice cream store in the middle of the desert in a town just southwest of St. George had to close because it couldn't sell ice cream in the summer when it's 110 degrees. The Hawaiian Poke Bowl is in a nondescript strip mall. But the owner, Roberta Gilbert, a Hawaiian native from the island of Oahu who knows her community and demographics, offers the best homemade poke. People driving on Interstate 15 between California and Salt Lake City make it a point to stop there, including people who are not fans of poke but love the Hawaiian Poke Bowl.

This is a phenomenon, not marketing. It is hard enough to find the right place, and many times that includes the luck of the draw. But Roberta offers great recipes and knows what she is doing. This is part of choosing your cuisine and people coming to your location. This is what everyone's trying to re-create, and it's almost impossible.

I am going to focus on researching and obtaining the best location for a brick-and-mortar restaurant. There are the options of ghost kitchens and food trucks, but those come with its own set of challenges.

Finding a Restaurant Location Is Like Finding Your Home

There will be several commercial realtors that represent different properties. Their names and contact info should be on the leasing signs in front of the shopping centers. Feel free to call them; it doesn't cost you anything. Sit down with them, but be wary of what they're saying, because their objective is to lease the property to you to make a commission. Make sure you tell them what you're looking for, and get options. There may even be places where some of the realtors know the business is about to close or wants to get out of its lease. Realtors know landlords who have restaurant properties they want to lease even though the property might not be listed yet. These are called *pocket listings*. It is always good to reach out to several realtors to get many options.

When you are meeting with realtors, you need statistics. You can go online or the library and get crucial demographic statistics. These include:

- How many people live in the city, on the street, and in the vicinity where you will open the restaurant?
- How many people work in the city where you will open the restaurant?
- What are the traffic counts on the street?
- What's the ethnicity of the neighborhood?
- What are the age groups?

Meet with two or three different realtors, and even go to lunch, since they will probably buy because they want to make the sale or lease the place. Remember, they are not doing you a favor. You are their client now and in their database, whether you use them or not. If you're successful, they will give you a lot of information about the location, area, demographics, and traffic flow. They will also provide you with information outside of what is available on the internet, like a secret of the trade.

You may want to open a new restaurant built from the ground up. As detailed in Chapter 1, if you have $25,000 to over $100,000 to open a restaurant, a third-, fourth-, or fifth-generation restaurant space for lease is more feasible and will save you thousands of dollars if it is the right place for you.

Traffic, Parking, and ADA Accessibility

What about parking and accessibility? Years ago I consulted with a restaurant on Tropicana Avenue, north of the airport, in Las Vegas. It was located next to an off-strip hotel in a strip mall, but accessibility was difficult at best. If you drove west on Tropicana Avenue, you could enter the parking lot easily. But Tropicana Avenue in that area has a cement median with no turn lanes into the retail center if traveling east. You would drive east past the restaurant past the next major street, Paradise Road, which is southbound only. You would have to drive to University Center Drive Street to turn north, then drive half a mile to Harmon Avenue, turn north onto Paradise Road, and then drive south on Paradise Road to pick up Tropicana Avenue going west. If you thought that was a lot to read, try explaining those directions to someone over the phone or in a text.

What about valet? There are some places with restaurant space to rent that is only valet and other places that don't offer valet. Is the location safe, especially if people need to park and walk? While people love the proverbial hole in the wall, they want to feel safe and be comfortable during their time there and while parking their car.

What about restrooms? How do you feel about sharing restrooms with other businesses, which is part of the design of malls and other multi-retail centers? If it is a private restroom, is one compliant with the Americans with Disabilities Act? You want to find a location that is ADA compliant with ramps and restrooms, since that is part of the certificate of occupancy. Also, another trend is a diaper-changing station in restrooms as well as gender-neutral restrooms.

These are considerations, and areas you need to research and really get information about before making a decision. For example, the Arts District in Las Vegas has become a thriving culinary community, but parking is limited because of the age and infrastructure of the neighborhood. Since rideshare is very popular with the demographic groups that go to the neighborhood and eat in these restaurants, parking is not an issue. The area is always busy and bustling, whether on a Sunday afternoon or a Wednesday night. Actually, every day of the week, the places are filled with customers, and these restaurateurs made the right decision for what they are offering.

Realtors can help with information about traffic flow and foot traffic. Remember, just because the location is in the middle of an area with thousands of people driving or walking by, that does not mean they're going to stop.

Are Nearby Businesses a Help or Hindrance?

Let's look at a strip mall, well maintained, on a busy street with a beautiful space that was leased as a restaurant. Businesses in the mall include a dry cleaner, a postal store, and other retail outlets. Are they comparative to the clientele you want for your restaurant? Realtors can tell you how many people come to the shopping center and how much foot traffic there is. But the businesses are closed around dinnertime. You see unlimited parking spaces. Let's say 75,000 cars drive by—that doesn't mean they are stopping. If the speed limit is 40 miles per hour, people are not going to stop on impulse. Is this still the right location for you?

Another important factor is what direction the location faces in terms of the sun. If it faces east or west, does the sun shine directly into the restaurant? If it's shining into the restaurant all afternoon, it can become hot and affect customers. Nobody likes the sun in their eyes, so find out that information.

Let's use the example of opening a Filipino restaurant. You find a great location in a shopping center with a seafood market that caters to Filipinos and other Asians. Your intuition tells you that it makes sense to open an international restaurant in a shopping center that has an international market. Still, meet with real estate professionals who represent commercial properties, to find out the statistics.

Past Performance Is No Guarantee of Future Results

Something else to consider is that just because there was once a very successful restaurant in the location doesn't mean your restaurant in that same space will be successful.

A perfect example was the updating and rebranding of a successful Mexican restaurant that had been operating as a staple in the community since 1935. A new owner took over the property in 2014 and revamped everything. The owner was connected politically and knew congresspeople, senators, the governor, and others in the political arena. The plan was that it would become the new hot spot for movers and shakers to meet and eat.

It didn't happen.

For every old-school place in the country, duplication doesn't always work today. What made The Rainbow on Sunset in Hollywood, Katz's Deli in New York, and The Pines of Rome in Bethesda, Maryland, special can't be transferred automatically.

One of my favorite Italian restaurants is a place called Amalfi Restaurante in Rockville, Maryland, that is an anomaly in a commercial district. The restaurant itself is on the back end of a warehouse building. There is minimal parking. Customers have to park in front of somebody else's building or on the street. Sometimes customers block each other with stacked parking. But the restaurant offers the most phenomenal white pizza and pasta dishes.

The glasses are the little juice-size cups, and the décor is old maps and fake plants. Still, I learned a lot from the owner, Moe, and his wife, Teresa, who spent hours with me. It is just an unbelievable place. It has warmth, service, and the greatest Italian food ever. I conducted meetings, celebrated birthdays and special occasions, and even brought dates there—and if my date didn't like it, I knew she wasn't the woman for me.

Unfortunately, you can't re-create Amalfi Restaurante. The reason it is so good is that the food is terrific and the service is excellent. You walk in there and feel like you are the most important person in the world.

You have to make your own magic.

Will You Be My Neighbor?

One demographic to consider are neighborhoods with residents.

For example, if you want to open a kosher restaurant, you need to find a location close to the Orthodox Jewish community. But if you want to open an Irish or Italian restaurant, people of all ethnicities eat the cuisine. Look at how many people become honorary Irish on St. Patrick's Day and proud of it. If it is a working-class, meat-and-potatoes neighborhood, upscale vegan food might not be what the residents want when they dine out.

My degree is in urban development, but the reality is that statistics will not tell you what's going to be successful. So let's talk about demographics, including potential places surrounded by offices, sports arenas, and convention centers.

I was working on a deal where the principles operated private airports with multiple locations in Florida. They approached me about needing a restaurant in a private airport. Patrons could look across the field and see all the planes flying in and out. My thought was that the concept was fun and the restaurant had a unique view. But then I realized that people who are using a private airport either board their planes and leave, or disembark and go home. As for the community, patrons would have to drive out of their way to an airstrip to have dinner. The destination would have to really ramp up its food and service to be successful.

At the time of publication, a new stadium for the Raiders is being built in Las Vegas. People are approaching me about opening a restaurant with a drive-through close to the stadium. It is not guaranteed to be the moneymaker everyone assumes it would be due to location. Out of 365 days in a year, there will be 18 games, possibly 20; so doing the math, there would be only 20 days to grab customers coming from the stadium. Another point is that this particular stadium is being designed for guests to come by rideshare and public transportation, so that cuts your customer base if you are depending on people driving to and from the stadium.

Convention centers are another demographic. In Sandy, Utah, there's a convention center with a professional soccer stadium and field in close proximity. When I drive past it, I see the restaurants, and usually they are empty. Just because the location is close to a convention center doesn't mean you will have a steady stream of customers. You will really need to calculate how many days a week the restaurant will be busy.

There are restaurants that make their profits off the convention trade. These restaurant owners don't care if they're dead in the off season. They don't reach out to the locals because they make bank with all the conventioneers. But the restaurants have been in business for a very long time and have a customer database of returning conventioneers.

Locations like sports arenas and convention centers present the problem of running out of food on the days with patrons. Personally, I'd rather have a slow and steady business. It's challenging to maintain a thriving business in a location catering to high numbers of patrons for a few days.

I have always calculated that you need to have 3,000 paid customers in your database to keep a business going with any chance for success. Those 3,000 customers need to remain consistent, and with seasonal locations, you can't build loyalty for customers to return. It would be hit or miss instead of building a steady business with a chance to grow.

Do Not Sign Anything Yet

Do not sign any lease or exclusive contract. Do not get locked into a contract with a realtor looking for a place for you. Again, I am going to repeat it: do not sign any contract or lease.

Now the List Is Getting Shorter

Right now, you should have a list of five or six places. Take that list and dissect the details such as traffic flow, parking, accessibility, cleanliness, and the community.

If you are opening a pizza place, is it close to an Italian restaurant? Do you cross that location off your list? Just because it's a beautiful place full of restaurant equipment, if one of the busiest Italian restaurants in the city is two doors down, it won't work for you. Or will it? Have you checked their menu?

Beyond all of your research, use your intuitiveness. Your gut is going to tell you whether it's right or wrong. Don't avoid that. Listen to what you're telling yourself. You will find every reason in the world to contradict what your intuition is telling you. Do not do that. Listen to yourself.

When a place is not right, walk away, no matter how awesome the deal is or the place looks.

Don't try to come up with another concept to compete, such as an Italian steak house. Do not change your plan over a location.

Some people get stuck on the location concept of "I have a restaurant concept, and I want the location in a specific area of the city."

Then do it.

In that case, you don't need this book; you need more money. But sometimes you can find a great restaurant in an expensive place because the landlord or realtor is not able to rent it; it's just sitting there, and the landlords/property managers want to get somebody in the space. Your idea might be what they want, so it doesn't hurt to ask.

Three Is the Magic Number

Now you need to pick three locations.

You know the whys; you have narrowed down the locations based on demographics, what people are saying, research, and what the health department has advised, because they have excellent insight on locations. Friends, realtors, liquor distributors, vendors, and many other people in the hospitality industry can help with your market insight and location.

For example, there was a fantastic restaurant space in an upscale retail center surrounded by several upper-middle-class and luxury neighborhoods. There was plenty of parking, it was easily accessible, and the building was beautifully designed. When the first restaurant that opened in that space failed, a restaurateur snapped it up and opened a totally unusual place with a different vibe and cuisine. That restaurant also closed in a short period of time. Then a chef found the space, leased it as a third-generation restaurant, and launched his place with a huge grand opening. Within a year, the chef changed the name of the restaurant because the original name was too similar to another restaurant in the community and customers went there instead. He also changed the decor and cuisine. His restaurant closed within a short period of time. Today that space has been transformed into an animal hospital.

Had the restaurateur or chef researched the space, I am certain realtors, liquor distributors, vendors, and people also leasing in the retail center could have given some insight to why the first and second restaurants closed their doors after a relatively short time.

Talk to everyone who can give you input on your top three selections. You have a list of yes, why, and why not. This is where you need to listen to your intuition. Calculate your risk, and say okay; this should not fail because of the information you have analyzed.

Go for it.

Don't Sign Any Lease or Contract

You have more research to complete.

Competition—What They Are Doing Right and Wrong

Now that you have selected your top three locations, what do you do next?

Check out the competition for your cuisine in the three locations. Do not make the mistake of saying, "There's a hamburger place three doors down, but I am better." That is the path to failure.

Go into that place and any other place that is competition for you, and eat their food. Look at their prices, the quality of food served, the portion size, the presentation, and the décor. Check out the cars in the parking lot. Get their menus. What do they serve the food on—paper plates and disposable silverware, or china and metal silverware? Observe their customers. What's their service like, and do you feel that they are of service to their customers? Do you feel warm, welcome, and fuzzy when you enter the restaurant? Is this the demographic you want to reach?

Go on Yelp and other social media, look at photos of the food, and print them out. While you can take pictures of your own meal without being creepy, taking photos of everyone's food might raise someone's suspicion.

Create a war room. Buy a roll of tape, get everybody's pictures and menus, and tape everything on the wall. Study them; see what is right and what is wrong, and how you can do it better.

Next, check and print out the reviews, because this will become your handbook to success. You can read what people don't like, and plan to do it differently. This will be a lot of work. But if you take a wall, add your menu, and then track the competition and photos of pasta, fries, burgers, soup, salads, and steaks, you will get a good idea of what you need to do. You should have five or six different photos from the restaurants that are your competition for customers.

The big companies with franchises and chains are successful because they research everything, including the competition. Then they research it again.

That Costs Extra?

Remember when you purchased your first car from a dealership? You did your research and found the perfect make, model, color, and upgrades. You negotiated a fair price, got some extras added at the dealer's cost, and were happy with the price and monthly payments. Then came the paperwork with additional fees such as sales taxes, documentation, registration, extended warranty, and other state fees. You were sitting there ready to take the keys and walk out to your new car, and suddenly your payment increased by $200 if you rolled it into your loan, or you had to pay the additional fees up front.

Sticker shock!

If you think there are extra costs when buying a car from a dealer, then you are in for a rude awakening or big surprise (depending on how you look at it) when leasing a space for a restaurant.

Rent and Utilities

The first set of extra costs includes utilities, garbage, water, and sewage. With your list now down to three locations, this is when you need to check out those details.

Realtors will quote the rental price broken down by the foot, and then there's the debt, or *triple net* as they call it. Triple net means you have to pay the bottom-line price. For example, if the quoted rent is $1,200 a month, there is an additional cost of CAM fees (community fees), which includes the cleaning of the building and parking lot and possibly water fees. Sometimes your trash is part of the CAM fees, but you're going to be paying for it. Many times you need to lease your own dumpster and put it behind your restaurant. Fees can add up to 15% more, not including the utilities you are responsible for, such as electricity.

If you can build out the location, landlords will pay for some of the remodel and buildout. I have worked on deals like that, but you can't go overboard. Don't ask for marble floors, but many land-lords will help you because they want a successful business operating for any profit sharing or to raise the rent on other places if not freestanding.

I was recently offered a percentage deal. They wanted 20% of the gross, which is a lot of money, but this was in lieu of rent. I needed to look at the average rent percentage of a business. Find a good accountant, because every city's different.

So what is the percentage? When you're looking at the rent, typically it shouldn't exceed 6–10% of your gross sales. For every $100 you make (gross), then $10 is the highest amount to pay toward rent. For every $1,000 you make (gross), $100 is toward rent. So if you are looking at a place that wants $5,000 a month (before other fees and no profit sharing), you need to make $50,000 to justify that cost. Also remember that real estate and labor combined can make up 40%, which means that for every dollar you're making, 40 cents is going to cover labor and the real estate expense.

Ingredients, Menu Items, and Beverages

This is just the beginning of costs. Now let's look at the cost of foods, which you need to plan to keep at 20%. You are doing your research and moving forward to make sure you are doing this correctly. There are membership clubs that sell in bulk, Restaurant Depot, Chefs' Warehouse, Sysco, US Foods, and other broad-line distributors including local distribution companies. They may require you to have a reseller's license and business license. Plan on getting one, but not yet, since you haven't made a full commitment. But you still need to meet with their salespeople, bring your menu, and go through costs.

Remember, these are salespeople. They want your sale. It's not going to cost you to meet with them and get information. Get a day membership for membership clubs to check on prices; and, depending on your location, you may or may not be able to walk into places like Restaurant Depot without your license in hand.

Here's one example of food costs to consider. While making your own fries from potatoes is less expensive, what about the time and labor to required? Compare the two costs.

You now look at your expenses on a worksheet with your starting menu. Set it up as a spreadsheet with ingredients, and list your ingredients down one side of the column. List your vendors across the top, and write down the prices in between. Fill them in so you can see who's got the best prices for what you need. Eventually, you'll have to look into plateware, silverware, and equipment. But begin with food costs. Everything will go on the same spreadsheet.

Employee Wages

As for labor costs, restaurants commonly aim to keep that expense between 20 and 30% of the gross revenue. This needs to include worker's comp insurance (required), health insurance (if you are offering that benefit), social security, and other taxes. I would advise talking to someone knowledgeable about human resources requirements in the restaurant business.

What About Investors?

Let's talk about investors and investment. When you're planning your restaurant concept, a lot of money is involved. You are reading this book to find out ways to open a restaurant without needing a lot of money.

Many people will recommend that you find an investor or investors (look at the popularity of television shows such as *Shark Tank*). One huge plus is that you receive a sum of money to open your restaurant. But there are disadvantages, minuses, and warnings when using investor money.

So you have an excellent idea for a restaurant, you need the money to open it, and you found someone who will potentially finance it.

Do not make the mistake of thinking that as long as you own 51%, you are the owner, and you make all the decisions—or worse, if you own an equal percentage as the investors, that all of you will make decisions together. It will never end up working that way, even if, and I mean *if*, the investor agrees to be passive.

Remember, an investor's decisions may not align with your choices. Let's look at this from a debit and credit standpoint. The investor may make better decisions than you would personally make, for whatever reason. The investor can also make bad decisions. It is imperative, if you include investors, that you both understand what percentage of ownership the investor wants for their funding and what their role will be in the operation of the restaurant. Are they willing to be passive investors, or do they want to take on an active role? Are you ready to have the investor take on an active role?

Here is a perfect example of investors and expectations. Restaurateur Steve Kennedy opened a new restaurant with celebrity chef Wolfgang Puck. Each investor bought a certain amount of points in the restaurant, and each point equals 1% of 100% of that particular restaurant corporation only. A few of the small-percentage investors started to input ideas and dictate terms, and immediately wanted to see all the financials.

I have always been told that the smaller the investment, the larger the complaint rate. So it's the 80/20 rule, meaning 80% of the smaller investors are going to complain more than the 20% with the more significant investments. There is an aggravation factor that could derail you. Be aware of your opportunity cost in terms of time that you are using to simply manage the investors.

When you deal with investors, you need to know the percentage they're going to want for the investment and what the value is. How do you determine the value?

For example, let's say you want to spend $100,000 to open your restaurant. You find an investor to invest $10,000. Do they own 10% of the business? What is their role, whether you determine they own 10% (which is not necessarily the case) or a lesser percentage? While on paper (contract), they might not have the right to demand input for decision-making, this will not stop the investor from contacting you, the owner, and inundating you with questions, concerns, and complaints. Is that $10,000 really necessary to open your restaurant, or can you find another way to cut the budget and maintain the entire ownership without answering to anyone, even if they don't have the legal right to question you?

What about reimbursing investors, and the profit structure? Another question is that if the business fails, do you still owe the money to the investor, depending on the legal setup?

What if you personally know the investors? Many people raise capital, the business doesn't work out, and they find something else. Well, I would feel very guilty if someone I knew invested in one of my companies, and the business failed.

Another consideration is that many times, the landlord of the property being leased wants a percentage of the profits. Suddenly, your 51% is no longer over 50%. What about ongoing expenses? Does the investor agree with your technology or marketing expenses? What about your salary? You need money to live on, and investors may complain that you can "cut back" on your salary and put that money back into the restaurant.

For example, if you have 20 investors who have put their own money into the business, this makes them owners. Even at 1%, they're still an owner. My advice to you if you are considering investors is to talk to both an experienced accountant and an attorney.

I am not an advocate of using investors.

What About Borrowing Money?

Yes, borrowing money is another option, and you need to be prepared to pay that money back, whether you are successful or not. You need to have a plan. I'm not saying you're going to fail, because that's entirely against everything I believe in, and that is why I have written this book. But things happen.

If you've done all your planning and research, you should be successful. But even if you're not making as much money as you thought, sometimes it's hard to pay back a loan. Keep these things in mind, and do some heavy soul searching. Don't spend your entire inheritance to pay back loans when you can find other ways to open your restaurant.

I Am Ready to Sign My Name ...

I know you think you are ready, but you are not. You still need to read Chapter 3 about regulations and compliance. Once you have completed that chapter, then you will select the final location and sign the lease!

Final Thought

My philosophy is that if you are willing to take the time and make an effort, you will have a plan and can open that restaurant with a stake of $25,000 to $100,000. I have outlined some strategies in the previous chapter and will guide you in the upcoming chapters to make that dream a reality.

3 Red Tape

You are now rolling your eyes. You dread going to all of the governmental agencies, a lawyer's office (if you hire one), licensing agents, insurance agents, and any other official entity. You just want to open a restaurant.

First, enjoy this process.

Yes, embrace and cherish this activity. When you do your research, reach out to all the government agencies—especially the health department—since they are there to protect you, your staff, and your customers.

You are devoted to opening a restaurant and close to selecting the location. Now you need to step back and protect yourself.

See Your Name . . . on Many Legal Docs

While you're in the process of determining your location, your next step is to set up your corporation. Do *not* operate your restaurant as a sole proprietor. I don't care if it is "just a burger joint." You can get sued, and you need to protect your assets.

First, get an employer identification number (EIN) from the IRS. This nine-digit number is assigned by the IRS to identify the tax accounts of employers, even if you have no employees. It is free through the IRS by going online to irs.gov and filling out Form SS-4. You will also eventually have to file a certificate of occupancy and file a DBA ("doing business as") certificate with the proper government office.

You need to create either a corporation or a limited liability company (LLC). There are several websites to help guide you through this process. You can talk to someone at the Service Corps of Retired Executives (SCORE), a nonprofit organization offering mentorship and advice from retired, successful business people. Visit SCORE.org to find a location in your area. There are other business mentorship programs, including universities with programs and mentors who can advise you. In addition, the Small Business Association (SBA) lists resources at SBA.gov.

After setting up either a corporation or an LLC, using your EIN number, find a bank and open a business account. Check out websites, visit banks, and speak with one of their representatives. Once you have selected a bank with the best fees and you have a personal relationship with a banker, open the account.

The resources mentioned, SCORE and the SBA, will also be invaluable in guiding you through the licensing process. This process is different in each state, and these resources can help you navigate the legal landscape.

For example, in Nevada, you need to apply for a state business license for the corporation as soon as you begin to conduct business, and before you apply for a local business license.

Before you can apply for a local business license, you will need to decide on the location. That will help you to determine what jurisdiction governs it, whether county, city, or township. One crucial point is that you can use a registered licensed agent's address for the corporation or LLC, but if the corporate address is in a different jurisdiction than the location of the restaurant, there will be more licenses. There are companies that specialize in providing services for small business owners, including registered licensed agents to represent corporations.

The Health Department Is Your Friend

Now you need to contact your local health department and obtain a list of what is required to pass the health inspection.

First, go online and find the health district website for your municipality. Make sure it is the official one—usually, it will be listed as [*name*].gov. Read the information available.

I advise you to visit in person; you should be able to call and make an appointment. The people who work at the health department are very helpful. They want your restaurant to succeed. They want a thriving business that serves good food in a safe, sanitary environment in their community.

During this visit to the health department, you will not be speaking to the specific health inspector who will eventually inspect your restaurant. You will be talking to other health department staff members.

You should begin to build relationships with these people. That is the operative word—they are *people*. I still know the names of assistants, receptionists, and other support staff. I made sure to let everyone know that my goal was to be compliant with all health department regulations and keep my staff and customers safe.

Now, when I go to the health department in any city where I have established a restaurant, the staff knows my name, a couple of people hug me, and I can accomplish my purpose. If I walk into a restaurant and bump into a health inspector I know, I always get a big hug. Don't freak out when you see the health inspector doing an inspection. For example, if I am using the wrong temperature on a piece of equipment, this inspector will inform me without writing me up, since the inspector knows I will immediately correct the temperature.

I am not suggesting bribery or gifts. They are not interested in food as a bribe. What I am advising you to do is to learn and use their names, and get to know them. This is how relationships are developed. No, don't stalk them on social media, but you should always be looking up profiles just to get an idea of the people you want to work with closely.

I have the personal cell phone numbers of many inspectors, so if, for example, the freezer stops working, I can call them to see how long I can keep the food and remain compliant. They want to help me, and they want to help you. It's their job because the last thing any health department in any municipality wants is an outbreak of foodborne illness. That reflects on them, and then you become the villain.

If you are vigilant about health compliance, there should be no foodborne illness. Remember, the wholesaler, distributor, vendors, and manufacturers where you buy your food to serve to customers also have to follow the regulations of the health department for compliance. If you and the suppliers meet the compliance level, the result is that people will come to eat at your restaurant, and you can trust the food being served.

I know that you hear horror stories because people think the health department inspector's sole purpose is to shut a restaurant down. That is not true. Your restaurant is being inspected to keep your food healthy for the community. Health department inspectors are the people who make sure any food you feed to customers, including children, is not tainted—which could cause illness or, in the worst-case scenario, someone's death.

The health department and its inspectors are not your enemies.

Stop the mindset that the health department makes a profit when you spend money on proper equipment and other modifications. A successful restaurant that meets its standards is good for them and the community. Get your ego out of it. This is not a test of your will.

They will happily give you the requirements, including grease trap, hood, three-compartment sink, unique wipeable walls, proper flooring, and other areas. Also, it is crucial to find out if you can purchase the equipment used or it has to be new. This is essential information when negotiating your lease and specifying who will handle upgrades of equipment to meet the health department code.

The Final Decision—Location—Is Approaching

Now you have your list, and you can really inspect the location. You can determine what equipment is offered and what needs to be replaced. You can negotiate with the landlord or property manager about what equipment and other areas they will upgrade. Also, where the equipment is placed is essential. For example, you need to find out how far the dishwasher needs to be located from food preparation.

There are restaurant consultants out there, but many do not have the proper information. A famous Los Angeles deli opened a restaurant in Las Vegas and ultimately failed due to misinformation from a consultant.

The kitchen was beautiful, and everything was brand new and top of the line. While I am assuming that the licensing and permits were in order, this consultant didn't know how to flow staff with food service and cleanup in the dining room. The consultant also didn't understand how everyone can work in a commercial kitchen without running into each other. People were all over each other trying to get ingredients because the setup was poorly executed.

There is one big area to consider: grease, if you are going to grill or fry anything. You need to check with your municipality to see what grease inceptor devices are approved for commercial businesses. In older retail centers, the pavement has been ripped up, and many times the pipe has been removed. In the past, many restaurants used a portable grease trap in the kitchen.

I've looked at some restaurants where everything appeared to be perfect, and it was just too good to be true. After investigating, we found a pipe for the wastewater, but then we looked at the grease inceptor system. That was the problem with the beautiful restaurant location we were considering: the grease trap machine was spinning and pumping water, and then someone had to dump it. Many municipalities no longer allow a portable grease trap. Sometimes landlords know this but don't share the information.

Ready for a Drink?

If you plan to serve beer, wine, and/or spirits, there is another process you will have to embrace: obtaining a liquor license.

You could possibly find a space with a liquor license that may or may not be grandfathered to the next business. State websites have sections for business licensing divisions and list general information for alcohol licenses. You can hire an attorney specializing in liquor licenses; that can get expensive, but you will be better protected. Also, ask the staff at the licensing department. Never *assume* that what the landlord, real estate agent, or your friend is telling you is the correct information. Only the licensing board can definitely tell you if a license is transferable.

Getting the license will probably require a background check. There might be a requirement to provide financial information. If necessary, check out fees for attorneys and others who specialize in licensing, but find one offering a flat fee.

Protection Equals Insurance

You need to protect yourself, and that is why you have insurance.

Your potential landlord will give you a list of insurances you and your business need to carry. These insurances only cover the landlord's potential losses. You still need the protection of insurance in case of a catastrophe or other problems such as if somebody chokes or a customer slips in the bathroom.

You need to find a corporate insurance person who works with insurance companies that specialize in covering restaurants. Your personal insurance agent might be able to give you some referrals. There are also local and state restaurant associations that will refer members. Remember that these associations may not refer you to somebody who is the best or can find the best rates in premiums and coverage; they're going to refer you to someone who is a dues-paying member. Organizations vet their members, but do your due diligence and research them as well.

When you speak to potential agents, explain that you are opening a restaurant. You may have the desire to mitigate your costs, but lawsuits are much more costly than the premium for the proper amount of coverage to protect you and your business.

Ask questions to make sure you are adequately covered, especially if alcohol is involved. What if a customer is served alcohol at the restaurant and then leaves, driving his or her own vehicle, and gets into an accident? What if a customer buys a sandwich and, while eating and driving at the same time, causes an accident? How will the restaurant be covered if the restaurant owner or a staff member is included in a lawsuit or the driver is charged criminally?

Your own insurance is a necessity. However, while you don't want to be underinsured, there are different rates, and you don't need to be overcharged.

Get estimates and study them. Find out if you need to add more insurance if you have a liquor license, since state regulations will require you to carry a certain amount of coverage. Find out what each agent can offer and what insurances they recommend you carry for your protection.

These are safeguards to protect your livelihood, your dream, and yourself. The proper insurance coverage may cost you a little more. So you sell some more food to cover these costs; in the end, it will be fine, since you will be protected.

Music Can Add to Appetites and Legal Problems

You love music, and you want to feature live entertainment, play recorded music in the background, or both, in your restaurant.

Along with everything else, you need music licensing rights to play music in public, as regulated by BMI (BMI.com) and ASCAP (ASCAP.com). To play music publicly, whether recorded or live, you must have a license. Copyright laws require retailers, restaurants, and other for-profit businesses to get permission from songwriters and composers to play their music publicly. Both organizations will help guide you, the restaurateur, get the proper licenses.

Do *not* think you can play one of the streaming services and avoid paying for a music license. These songs are protected under BMI and ASCAP, and you will be heavily fined. In a live music situation, do *not* make the mistake of accepting the entertainers' word that you don't need a music license when they perform. It is your establishment, and *you* are the one who is responsible and will be fined.

Do you want to showcase live music? You need to research entertainment licensing and entertainment tax. You need to check with your municipality to see if you will be charged a flat fee or a per-person entertainment tax. Here is the caveat—if your municipality does it by occupancy (per person), you will pay whether people attend the show or not.

Let's use an example of an occupancy rate of 150 people allowed in your establishment at one time. You book your second cousin twice removed, because all of your relatives and family promise to attend and support a member of the family. You are charged a per-person entertainment tax for an occupancy of 150. Only three people show up. Guess what? You still have to pay as if 150 people attended.

Remember, you can always offer live entertainment later. There are also many royalty-free sites online where you can select music, but make sure the music can be played in a commercial establishment. You don't want to be sued for infringement.

What's Your Sign?

Of course, you need signage, which involves one-time fees.

At this point, you need to ask the landlord about the requirements for signage. You will need to hire a sign company. Services that you need for certain that should be included in their fee are design and installation, and submitting proper permits to the proper department. The company should be able to create graphics and schematics and submit to the appropriate department. This is one time you should not go a la carte but rather should find a full-service sign company. As to what should go on the sign, that will be discussed in Chapter 4.

Selling Merch and Offering Entertainment

If you're going to have merchandise and food items for sale, you need a resale permit. This includes t-shirts, coffee cups, caps, and other merchandise. You will probably want to include your logo on many of your items, and I talk about that in Chapter 8 about branding.

You want your restaurant to have a casual vibe, and offering a place to play billiards or pool will add the right element. In some municipalities, you might need a license to offer pool tables. There might also be an entertainment tax, so check with your local and state offices that handle licensing.

This Is a Special Time

I like to enjoy this process of getting the required licenses, and that's what makes it so special. You will go from one office to another. Most of the time, you won't have to wait in long lines, but you might in some places. You may have to pay a couple of hundred bucks in fees, but what an experience for you to go from department to department and really learn about the process. If you work with the administrators, they're going to help you; and, more importantly, they want you to succeed. It's all set up for you to succeed. It is not about the money, although fees are involved, and you might feel over-whelmed. The process is set up to make sure everything is covered, including dotting your i's and crossing your t's.

One of the important licenses includes the health department and the final certificate of occupancy, and you can't get that until you have your equipment. But you can prepare. The key to this whole thing is preparation.

You might get frustrated at certain points when you're trying to line up licenses. Every municipality is different, and when you've talked to the federal, state, and local tax people, they may have sent you in various directions. Unfortunately, at this point, the process is not accessible and easy. No one has a set list of things for you to accomplish. But you are determined and passionate about opening a restaurant.

Think of this process as a positive experience. It's an exercise toward your success. It's not a pain in the ass. It's not someone trying to stick their hands in your pockets. The people working in the various departments are there to help you with consultations and advice.

When you meet with them, ask them what they think of your ideas. Ask them what you need to do to accomplish your goals. This is the process. They're going to tell you honestly if your plans meet regulations. They deal with this 24 hours a day, since inspectors sometimes pop in at night.

This is your business. You're staking your life on it. Lose your ego, ask the questions, write down the answers, study the process, and then figure it out like a puzzle. All this licensing will help you in the end. That's why the process was established. It was not put in place to hurt you or your restaurant. Do you want to walk into an office building and worry that the lights could fall on you? Do you want to drive down the street and plummet into a big hole where roadwork is being done, because there are no proper regulations to guide drivers?

This is why there are systems to keep you and your customers safe. There is nothing wrong with compliance. This is not a place where you want to be a rule-breaker.

Save the rule-breaking for your marketing. Compliance will create the deepest business relationships you can make, because when a health inspector walks through your door, you will know them, and they will know you want to work with them.

This might be called red tape, but I love it. You should enjoy it as well, to make this one of the best experiences of your new life.

4 The Dream Becomes Reality

Take a deep breath.

You have chosen a space based on your research and criteria. You are making a commitment. You are now ready to open a restaurant. There is still a lot of work to be done, but this is the make it or break it moment.

Put a Signature on It

You have the lease, and now you need to sign it.

First you need to review it. I urge you to have an attorney review it as well. As I have mentioned in previous chapters, there are legal services that charge a small fee to review a lease. I am not an attorney, but I also advise you not to sign a lease giving a personal guarantee that the business will remain operational during the length of the lease. A personal guarantee is a written, legal promise that you will personally pay the lease in its entirety. This means if the business defaults on the lease, then you, the business owner, will be personally responsible for repaying the complete amount of the rent for the term of the rental agreement. You don't want to be liable if something happens. While I have been a part of many success stories, life happens, so avoid that kind of guarantee.

I have witnessed prospective lessees offer two to three months of security deposit instead of a personal guarantee. The extra payment allows the landlord more time to lease the real estate if you have to close the business before the lease is up. This way, you are not responsible for the term of the lease.

Once everything is approved, you sign the lease, the landlord ratifies it, and you have a legally binding contract and a key. You are on your way to opening a restaurant.

I Now Pronounce You Restaurant and Restaurateur

You are living the mission, the value, and the idea. You had the mission of opening a restaurant. Now your mission is almost accomplished. It is nearly opened.

However, you are not standing in a restaurant where the dining room is completed, the kitchen is fully operational, the staff is in place, and, boom, you are ready to open the doors to eager patrons.

What's really next?

You have a key to an empty restaurant space.

It's time to take out your pad and pen or device and start to create a timeline for when you want to open and a list of things you need to get done.

First, find your kitchen equipment and schedule the installation, and locate all of your kitchen essentials and utensils. Begin planning with the health department for their inspection. Your timeline will speed up, since you must have a clean, up-to-compliance kitchen. Make sure you have no food stored in the kitchen before the inspection. If you do have any food stored in the kitchen, the inspector will make you throw it all away in front of them. Get all of your licenses, now that you have an address. Set up times for the walkthrough of the space.

The inspectors will want to see how the gas lines are set up or if the kitchen is all-electric. They will check the sinks to make certain they are working correctly. Health and sanitation supplies will be checked, and you will need to demonstrate how they will be discarded. Everything will be confirmed to be sure your space is Americans with Disabilities Act (ADA) compliant for the building's certificates. Since you did your research, you know what needs to be done.

As soon as you get your final approval from the health department and your building occupancy, you can focus on other areas.

Pleasing to the Eye and Appetite

Along with the kitchen, you have to build out the front of the house to be functional and aesthetically pleasing.

The design of the space depends on the type of restaurant you are opening. Certainly, upscale places need more formal interior design. But if it is casual or you want the warmth of a family dining room, you can create much of the aesthetics on your own. This will be one giant package; it doesn't have to be done professionally, and you don't have to pay anybody to do it. You wrote down everything during your research. You will rewrite it several times, and, by the end, you'll have your vision. Look back at your design ideas. Then, start a new action list of what you need to do.

Always remember, the design of the restaurant is not just about the walls or lighting. It also involves the textures of the napkins and placemats. It determines the type of silverware and plating. What kind of tables and chairs will fit? Will you have booths or a counter? What about an open kitchen?

Keep your brand in mind, and don't be afraid to experiment with color. Use different hues and color tones to establish an image for your restaurant, creating the right ambiance and stimulating the customers' appetites. Choosing the right color can make diners feel a wide range of emotions. Be strategic with your color choices, and use them to convey the dining experience based on your brand.

For example, according to The Balance: Small Business (thebalancesmb.com), colors that don't work well for restaurants include purple and blue. Ironically, blue is usually selected as a well-liked color in the US and is thought to have a calming effect. However, not many natural foods are blue (except blueberries). Blue and purple foods are usually dyed and subconsciously affect diners' appetites.

As you are in the process of creating, this is the perfect time to sit down with vendors and see what they advise and what options they can offer you. It is important to remind yourself that you may or may not buy something from this vendor, but at least you'll see all the options available. Visit restaurant supply houses, including those that sell used items. For example, if you are considering using bone china, you might find a great deal in a place that sells used restaurant supplies.

There are warehouses offering equipment, silverware, plateware, and other items. However, these types of places provide minimal customer service. You are expected to know what you want to purchase. This is why I recommend keeping notebooks of pictures and research as well as speaking to vendors. You have many choices, and you will determine the best places to purchase what you need. With so many online options and national classifieds available, you can really save money. Now is also the time to bring in your photos of plates or silverware that you liked at other restaurants. You can take your notebook or device and check out your lists of equipment and supplies in the restaurant supply warehouse setting.

This is why you did research, created notebooks with notes and pictures, and studied your own experiences: so that when this moment arrives, you have an excellent idea of what you want for your restaurant and can make a final decision.

Beauty Is in the Eye of the Beholder and License Holder

As for décor on the walls, many restaurants feature art created by local artists. But be forewarned if you purchase any artwork online or at a retail center, including discount or big box stores: you might need permission to display that art in a commercial venture.

When I walk into restaurant franchises and see antique pieces on display, I wonder about the legality of it. One item I see quite a bit is Moxy Root Beer. My friend's grandfather developed Moxy Root Beer. Could my friend's grandfather walk into a restaurant, see the likeness and image of Moxy Root Beer in the restaurant, and then contact the owner about trademark infringement? Maybe. If someone has enough money and wants to follow through, they can pay for an attorney to sue the owner of the restaurant for displaying something they created. I would avoid any problems and only display licensed and original work.

Personally, I would be annoyed if I walked into a place and saw covers of *Food & Beverage Magazine* blown up and on the walls. Of course, if I featured you or your restaurant on the cover, I would be thrilled to have that cover showcased on the walls. However, you always need permission. There is an implied endorsement when a magazine cover is featured on a wall of a restaurant. Be safe, and get it in writing.

A Menu Is More Than a List

There are many aspects to making a good impression on your customers, and one of them is the menu. It is also your key sales tool and is integral to the décor. Even before a customer begins to read the menu, it can capture their attention, or it has become a lost opportunity to make a good impression. Even worse, a poorly designed menu can make a wrong impression, even if it might be subconscious.

The menu is truly the first tactile thing the customer touches when they go to a restaurant. So what is it you want them to feel? What message are you trying to convey? When you touch the menu (not read it), how do you envision your restaurant?

A menu is more than a list of food and beverages being offered and their prices. What does it look like visually? What does it feel like in your hands? What does the menu say to the customers? Does the menu capture your vision? What is the feeling you want your patron to have when you hand them the menu?

For example, when you go to eat in a Chinese restaurant, their staff might hand you a giant laminated menu. There are usually lots of pictures with many options, and I think that's fun for that type of restaurant. There is a national chain that features a 50-page menu with spiral binding; it has pictures, and the choices seem endless. This menu fits with this chain.

Some higher-end restaurants give their customers a menu on one page of parchment paper with options available for the evening. Other restaurants provide a menu on one piece of copy paper with the dishes offered for the day. These restaurants print the menu every day since it changes daily. Some Italian restaurants have menu boards that are more cost-effective but create a certain feeling. It is all about telling your customers your story and using it as a tool, not merely what a customer can order.

I am a big fan of The Palm Restaurants. For many years, they used a fantastic, oversized paper menu, and I just loved it. It was amazing. It was a thicker paper, and my go-to waiter, Dutch Mohler, would come over and say to me, "What is this? Is there a stain on this menu? Give me that menu," and then he would rip it up in front of me and hand me a brand-new one. Now that's a great way to interact with your customers.

Suppose your restaurant sells barbecue with a décor of checkered red and white tablecloths and hard melamine plastic plates that look like paper plates. What about the menu? It could be fun newsprint.

I have gone to eat in restaurants where the feeling I got when I was handed the menu was that it was just a list of what I could order. Make sure the menu works with the décor and the feeling you are creating in your restaurant, because being handed the menu is all part of the experience.

Tempt the Appetite with the Menu

You have decided on the type of menu, and now it is time for the actual content. Again, how intricate to make your menu depends on the kind of restaurant you are going to open.

Unless you plan to use a one-page menu that you will print on your own, you should have a graphic artist design your menu, especially if you will be using it for a longer period of time. A menu is a selling tool as well as a marketing tool. You can reach out to universities and colleges offering classes in graphic design for student interns. You can also find freelance graphic designers online who offer reasonable rates.

Have the graphic artist lay out your menu by category. Each category should have five to seven selections including appetizers, entrées, soups, salads, desserts, and beverages. Apply this method to categories with at least six to eight items.

If you have done your homework, you have determined the gross profit of each item on your menu. The menu formula is simple. The first menu item listed should have the highest gross profit, and the last should have the second highest. All other menu items are placed between the first and last items. Here is the math. If 80,000 guests order from your menu each year, that will give you 80,000 chances to sell those guests a higher-profit item. Just adding $2 more profit per meal could lead to additional revenue of $160,000 per year.

Let's discuss logos and trademarks, since they are part of the menu. Do not go online and "find" something to use as your logo or trademark. If you want a logo, have an original one created, and then trademark it. The same is true with a tagline.

What is a tagline or a slogan? Think of fast food chains and the phrases used in commercials that you can remember. That is a tagline. If you choose to have a slogan or a tagline, make sure it is catchy and about your brand.

A chef in Las Vegas used a simple tagline for years. Then he received a cease-and-desist letter from an attorney. Apparently that particular tagline had been trademarked, and when the trademark owner of the slogan visited Las Vegas, he was stunned to hear his tagline being used by someone else commercially. You don't need to receive any correspondence from an attorney over a logo or slogan; you can search for any logo or tagline online and see what comes up.

As for the individual menu items, customers are looking for gluten-free choices as well as acknowledgment of allergens. If you are going to offers details on the menu that an option is vegan, soy-free, gluten-free, peanut/nut-free, or plant-based, there are restrictions and rules—you can't just say "nut-free." There are official USDA logos that can be used if they fit.

If you are offering a brand-name product such as a beverage, make sure you can use their logo, and get it in writing. Let me repeat that: if you list a brand name anywhere in the restaurant or on the menu, be sure you offer the real thing, and get it in writing. Maybe at home you can pass off the store brand as the good stuff, but not in a restaurant.

A Picture Really Is Worth a Thousand Words

While Chapter 5 will go into detail about cooking and testing every recipe, you should already know what you will be serving in your restaurant.

You need photos for your website, for social media, and maybe even for the menu. They are important representations of your brand; I always try to hire a professional photographer.

Did you notice I wrote, "Hire a professional photographer"?

Yes, there are photographers who specialize in photographing food, and they are expensive, but they are worth it because they understand how to light food (which is very difficult), bringing out the best in color, texture, and appeal. It is a skill and an art, and those photographers with expertise in photographing food will charge a higher rate. However, there are ways to get professional photos at a fraction of the cost.

You can approach your potential vendors. Yes, *potential*, since you are still meeting with them to see if you will purchase inventory from them. Many of the prominent suppliers have kitchens to create recipes, allowing for photographs to be taken for your use. The vendors may even pay for the photoshoot if you are going to order from them. Remember that the more food you sell, the more you are buying from them. So it is to their advantage for you to represent the product that you are buying from them in the best possible way.

Here is the caveat—never lie just to get a free photoshoot. If you promise you are going to order inventory from them, follow through. If you say to them that you are just testing recipes, make sure everyone understands that, and that there is only the expectation of a potential sale. There is nothing wrong with letting them know you are on a budget. In order to make a sale, these vendors will look for ways for you to save money. It becomes in their best interest to help you.

Another way is to read local magazines and find out the names of the photographers published in that issue. Read about them on social media and their websites. I know of several restaurants that found photographers who wanted to add food shots to their portfolios. Usually, the photographer was paid in trade with gift certificates or a couple of meals in exchange for taking photographs for the restaurant owner's use. While shooting food might not be a particular photographer's specialty, they are professionals and can take good shots with digital cameras.

You can reach out to local schools, colleges, and universities that offer photography programs. These include educational outreach programs offered by high schools and colleges as well as programs for adults who want to learn a new skill but not a degree. There are also big camera stores offering classes for people who want to hone their skills; you can reach out to offer a chance for real experience. Social groups such as MeetUp.com offer another way to find people who want to improve their photography skills in exchange for a couple of meals.

People in these groups take photography very seriously. While photography might be considered a hobby or avocation because people work another job, you can receive some great photos from a skilled photographer and save money.

Do Not Ignore This Vital Statement

The next paragraph is critical for you to read and understand the responsibilities and obligations of graphic artists.

It is not part of the job of a graphic artist to create content, proofread, or know what should or should not be included on a menu. It is up to you to make sure everything is correct. Yes, you can ask for help from others. In fact, I encourage it, since more eyes always catch errors. A graphic artist might point out any errors, but this is just to be helpful, not part of their services.

A great starting point prior to going to a graphic artist is to creatively write menu descriptions of each of your menu items. Talk to the chef and cooks about how they would describe the dishes. Ask them about the appearance and taste of each dish, and paint a picture with its look and taste. Use buzzwords such as rich appearance, encrusted, sautéed, buttery, tender, sweet, savory, rich, creamy, and succulent, and always mention the high-quality ingredients. Sometimes this description alone helps justify a higher price point.

Write the family backstory of the dish, and use ethnic names, which are always great to lend authenticity. Include the geographic origins of the ingredients.

I want you to get carried away and write entire paragraphs. Once that is done, begin to edit your descriptions down to a few short words that evoke the right emotions while keeping the descriptions short and easy to read. However, have your graphics team read the long descriptions, which can help in their creativity.

I am in the publishing industry, so here is an excellent example of why you need several people to proofread. Another magazine (no longer in publication) had seven people read and proof an issue before it went to the printer. Several of these people were trained writers and editors with years of experience in newspapers and magazines. The cover was beautiful, and everything looked great. Then came the big day when the magazines arrived from the printer, ready to be distributed. One of the partners, a man who did not have any training and had not proofed the magazine, looked over the issue and pointed to the table of contents. The word *Contents* had been spelled *Cotents*.

Even if customers don't catch a spelling or grammatical error, they will notice it subconsciously. Make sure everything is correct and that any logos or trademarks used in the menu are proper and can be included legally.

I also recommend that your menu be trademarked or copyrighted. You will need to talk to an attorney, but it may be worth doing it if your menu, logo, and tagline are creative and you want to keep them for your use only.

Dress to Tempt Those Taste Buds

Casting the wait staff and kitchen staff is covered in Chapter 5, but uniforms are part of the décor and your vision of the restaurant.

What's the look you are envisioning, especially in motion? There are aprons, white shirts with bow ties, denim shirts, and jeans. Do you want white or black shoes? You need to make wardrobe decisions for the back of the house, too. What do you want the chefs and kitchen staff to wear?

When I opened my hamburger places, I found 1940s-style uniforms with striped shirts along with hats with my logo. I also designed the logo and menu to capture that decade's feeling.

What hats does the kitchen staff wear? Since kitchen staff are required by law to cover their hair, they have to wear hats. What do those hats look like when worn by several people? Are they black baseball caps? Are they red? Is it a theme? Does it have your logo? Is it a 1940s baseball hat, or is it a hat capturing the theme of today? Do they simply wear hairnets? There are many options, but write down everything you have noticed and just keep the list flowing. Yes, use your yellow pad, notebook, or device.

What about name tags? It's all part of the uniform, and a name tag is another part of your vision. Some places have the staff use first names, and others have the staff use fun, made-up nicknames.

I was attending a business lunch at Miller's Ale House, and our waiter's name tag—which used his last name, Crowley—made an impression on me as a customer. When I asked about the name, this very engaging server told me about being called by his last name. There are also themed restaurants like Dick's Last Resort with funny, fake names. Some of the restaurants use white craft paper on the table, and the wait staff come up with a magic marker and write their name on the table. I know as a customer, I never forget it. It's fantastic, and this is one place that doesn't need name tags. However, a name tag can bring a sense of familiarity and also be used as a tool of engagement.

This is the time when you should be bringing out your notebook, since you should have been thinking about this for months. You are casting your restaurant with costumes to give patrons an experience. Remember, you are the director and executive producer.

As for purchasing uniforms (new or used), you will have to maintain the upkeep on them. If you hire a uniform company, it costs a little more, but the uniforms are cleaned and delivered, usually along with your restaurant linens.

How to Take an Order

Are you going to use electronics and technology? Will the servers go to the table, or will the customers pay up front? Will the orders be handwritten?

Personally, I love it when servers write out orders. I think it's the most refreshing, classiest thing ever. However, with your research, you should have decided on the best way to take an order at your restaurant.

You will need to decide what you are going to use for your point of sale (POS) system, if that is how you will submit orders and checks paid. There are vendors that sell POS systems, including your local bank, and you need to talk to them. You also need to ask for advice from your contacts in the food and beverage industry. You can attend expos and conventions for the food and beverage industry to find out more information. Remember, you can always upgrade, although upgrading can be costly. You want to consider efficiency, accuracy, and adding to the dining experience when a server takes an order.

There is a trend in some of the national chains to use tabletop devices and have the customer place their own order. Some restaurants will not accept cash for payment. There are online orders. Of course, the most significant trend is delivery, which will be covered in Chapter 8.

I believe in engagement and comradery, and that is why there should be interaction between the server and the customer. A tabletop device is impersonal, and with all the devices in our lives, we need human contact. A tabletop device can't determine how busy a kitchen is at the moment; and while it can "recommend" specials and specific dishes, how does a piece of equipment know how the food tastes?

Now is the time to make that decision. Remember, you can always change your method as well as upgrade if the time is right.

Everyone Has an Opinion

Up to this point, you have been planning methodically. You have been writing everything down on your yellow legal pad or device, and you're keeping track of all the information. (Remember to date it at the top in the upper-right corner and put the subject on the left side.) You have listed all the things that you have to get done.

You have received guidance from attorneys, accountants, restaurant designers, vendors, salespeople, food suppliers, and realtors.

Now I recommend that you talk to your peers in the food and beverage industry. Go online and look up different restaurant associations. Join forums and groups and read them, or maybe become a member. Find out who you think would be the best people in the restaurant industry to talk to about getting some advice. You are not asking them about what to serve and how to open a restaurant; you are going to sit down with someone, tell them what you have planned, and ask for any advice to make it better.

Remember, if you don't ask for help or advice, you're not going to get it. People love to help, and all you need to do is ask them.

Approach those who are not in competition with you with the same type of restaurant. You can find people who are retired from the restaurant business. And you can talk to people who have opened the same kind of restaurant but in a different city or state.

Here is the caveat—take everything someone tells you with a grain of salt, because everybody has a different motive for talking with you. Keep that in mind, and don't believe everything they say. However, listen and write it down. Once you have several ideas, brainstorm and role-play, and you will realize what works and doesn't work for you and your restaurant.

If you've hired a project manager, don't rely on them to make all the decisions. This is your baby, and ultimately, you need to make the decisions. If you do have a project manager, be prepared to redo many areas.

I've walked into many restaurants that were ready to open, and I could tell that everything was wrong with the business. For example, a wonderful, iconic delicatessen, restaurant, bakery, and bar, Canter's Deli, opened in Los Angeles in 1931. The restaurant licensed its name and concept to a restaurateur to expand into Las Vegas, opening in an upscale retail center with a second location on the Strip. They hired a consultant who completely changed the iconic menu and the interior style of the concept. Fans of the restaurant came in droves to eat their favorite dishes and found nothing familiar. Customers started complaining through social media and deterring people from coming to try the new locations. Both locations in Las Vegas closed in under a year. This is a perfect example of a restaurateur putting blind faith into a consultant and not taking control.

Bring together your family and your friends, and do a focus group. This will be different from "friends and family" day when you invite people to come to your restaurant as a dress rehearsal of the food and service. Offer some menu items, and listen to what they think and how they feel about your place. Do they want to eat there? Do they want to hang out there? Write down everything to review later.

Don't be shy about reaching out. This is not a time in your life or your future career for you to be shy. Step out of your box. Don't be embarrassed. If you don't know somebody, make the call anyway, and don't be afraid or take any rejection personally. Take your ego out of the equation.

Walking Through the Fire

To this day, I try not to assume the negative. I always reach out to anyone with the understanding that the worst thing that could happen to me is that they hang up (if I called them) or just ignore me.

There is one more way to be rejected: you can be told that no one wants or needs your business.

I started *Food & Beverage Magazine* while living in Washington, D.C., and I was confident this publication would be successful. I decided to move to Las Vegas to develop the magazine further in the western United States. Las Vegas was becoming a trendy new restaurant town with prominent chefs, and I wanted to be part of this new development in Sin City.

When I moved to Las Vegas, I didn't know anyone.

I attended UNLVino, an annual food and beverage event to benefit the University of Nevada, Las Vegas. It was there that I first met Larry Ruvo, the owner of the premier wine and spirits distributor in Nevada, Southern Wine and Spirits. He was wonderful to me. I told him about *Food & Beverage Magazine* and its mission to inform and help restaurateurs, investors, and chefs. I wanted to be a part of building and creating the food and beverage industry in Las Vegas beyond buffets and the then very popular 99-cent breakfast specials being offered on the Strip and downtown.

This man looked into my eyes and felt my passion. Ruvo had started his business on his own with help from his parents and their Italian restaurant. He had built his company into the biggest liquor distributorship in Nevada, and that included the Strip, downtown, and all the bars and restaurants outside of the tourists' area.

Ruvo became excited while speaking with me, and, without me even asking, told me that he would certainly advertise and do everything he could to help me and *Food & Beverage Magazine* succeed in Las Vegas.

It was an exhilarating and enjoyable experience. I had connected with Larry Ruvo, the king of the event, where everybody was desperate to get his attention. He had spent all this time with me and wanted to meet with me about the magazine.

He emphasized that I was to call his office and set up a meeting. So I called his office, not knowing what to expect. The staff knew who I was, had been expecting my call, and were very excited about the meeting.

On the day of the meeting, I walked into the conference room without knowing anyone except Ruvo.

I met Mike Severino, the chief marketing officer of Southern Wine and Spirits, who programmed all the spirit events with the casinos. I met Reno Armeni, a veteran in the liquor business, but I admit I didn't know his role in the company. The meeting was very overwhelming, with everyone dressed in their best suits. Ruvo literally marched me in, introduced me, and explained that he had another business meeting to attend. I clearly remember Ruvo telling everyone in the conference room that whatever I wanted, "Give it to him. I want you guys to talk through this." He left the room. At that point, I thought, "Wow, this is a home run. He just made my career. What a wonderful man!"

Pleasantries were exchanged, and then Armeni turned to me and said, "We don't need this f*****g magazine in this city."

Period.

Talk about a wind-leaving-your-sails moment. Within minutes, I fell from a euphoric high to a crushing low.

I actually started to sweat. What do I say? How do I respond to that? My ego wanted to get involved. I wanted to just get crazy.

I took a minute. I took a breath. I think maybe Severino was a little embarrassed. At that point, I told the room that I appreciated their input. I dug deep to maintain my composure.

I have to admit, I was defeated at the time. I invested every dime into building the magazine. But when you think you're going to come out with a home run and you come out as a loser, what happens? You build your character, and you realize the integrity of people, good and bad. I had to accept that it was a defeat, but I still had other options. This one time was not a home run, but that was okay.

Other distributors in town supported me, and I built some beautiful relationships as the business grew. It was almost as if I made better relationships because of the attitudes of the people I met at Southern Wines and Spirits.

I became very close with many people who worked at Southern Wine and Spirits, and they are lovely people. My relationship with Southern Wines and Spirits remained cantankerous, but it also became legendary.

One of the things I've learned is that if somebody is not paying you, you owe them nothing. I had to realize that these people were not supporting me and were working against me.

Through the magazine, I held many upscale events, sponsoring different liquor brands. If the brands were distributed through the company, there was always some kind of contention. Over the course of hundreds of meetings and lunches, the relationship remained stable, but the issues were never truly resolved.

Still, it was fun, and it drove me even harder to succeed. When people refuse to help, it can either be a ladder to your success or a roadblock. I prefer to call it a speed bump.

This occurred 20 years ago, and at times over the years I believed it was a setup for some weird reason. Regardless of anyone's opinion, I was determined that the magazine was going to be published and be successful. Over 20 years later, 12 million readers a month visit our website and read what I have to say. I have opened many successful restaurants. My biggest success is that you are reading this book.

The moral of the story is that in the end, you're going to get what people want to give you. Don't be offended by total rejection, because I believe I have no one to thank but those three men for much of my success. I made a commitment, and I fought, overcame, and created a lasting success. You can as well, and live your dream.

Take the good and bad, mix it all together, and then make your own opinion. Take all the information people are giving you, digest it, process it, and use it to your advantage.

Remember, the scenario that happened to me can happen to you. Still ask for guidance. You're not going to get everything you want—you will receive what people want to give you. It is up to you to become a success.

See Your Vision

This is really happening. You have created the mission, and now the vision is becoming a reality. There is much more for you to do; you are in the middle of your dream.

My question to you is this: do you love it?

The answer needs to be yes. You need to love this even with the headaches, mistakes, false moves, deadlines, and other challenges. You need to enjoy this process.

If you said a resounding "YES!" without thinking about it and can't imagine living your life doing something else, you are on the right track.

5 Your Restaurant Is a Stage

As you begin to staff up your restaurant, think about this as if you are the producer and director and are casting people to perform in your movie or play. Think about the culture you want to create in your restaurant and how everyone will fit. This includes the wait staff, chef, cook, bus people, and others. You are creating an environment where people will want to share special occasions, make memories, and remember eating in your restaurant as part of their life experience that they talk about for years.

After reading the next paragraph, close your eyes. Envision how your restaurant is going to be operated. What is your flow? Imagine what the customer will experience when they open the door to your restaurant. Who will they see? What will be said?

I am imagining that I see a beautiful smile greeting the customer. The wait staff is talking to everybody, especially the seated patrons. Everyone knows the customers' names if they have eaten there before, and the staff introduce themselves to all the customers dining there for the first time. The server remembers a returning customer's favorite dish. The entire team is helping everybody and working together. If there is a rush, one server will take care of another's table by acknowledging the patrons sitting there. Everyone is pouring the drinks, clearing tables, and making sure the customers have the best dining experience ever.

Now close your eyes and use your imagination.

Do you envision what I have envisioned for many restaurateurs? Can you see it in your mind, touch it, feel it, smell it, and hear it?

Now Create That Vision as a Reality

When you start hiring, remember, you need to hire team players. This is not about team-building experiences; this is about being of service to the patrons and each other. Everyone needs to understand your mission and value offered in the restaurant, including being of service to everyone. Again, that means each other, not just the customers.

Your job is to bring the customers to the restaurant. The only way they're going to come back after the first time is when everybody is working together and being of service.

Sometimes a customer will complain to a server about something, and that server can handle the problem. Rather than make a big deal with that complaint and bring the manager or even owner over to the table—or, worse, ignore the problem—the server can smooth it over and create the best dining experience possible. That is true teamwork, and that is the attitude you are looking for when hiring your staff.

The Auditions

First you made the plate (food), created the set (dining room), and completed the kitchen (backstage). Close your eyes, think of "actors" and "actresses," and this becomes the staffing. You're going to be casting your restaurant. Much like the opening scenes of a movie or the parting of the curtains, the greeter (formerly known as a hostess) will create the first human impression of your restaurant (the second is touching your menu).

Now you are casting your wait staff. Keep in mind that someone can perform as a great server at a French restaurant or a steak house and not at a hamburger place. Someone can sell a great meal but not know how to sell a great sandwich. First, you've got to think about what it is you're selling; because, in the end, it's all about sales. You need to understand the customer who is buying the food you are selling and hire servers who can sell it to the patron. You need wait staff and greeters who can really engage as well as sell menu items.

Make Sure Your Team Feels Like Partners

I don't call them employees. They are your *partners*, and they will be your face to the customers as well as your entire restaurant. They should feel that they are part of the ownership—not legally, but in terms of taking great pride in working in your restaurant. You are looking for staff whom other restaurateurs will try to poach or steal away, but the "partners" will say no because they love where they work. What a compliment to you when you hire people who feel that way about you and your restaurant.

One example is in a film starring Tom Hanks, *That Thing You Do!*, which takes place in 1964. The plot is about a band recording their first album in Los Angeles. The hotel where the group stays employs a person (then called a bellhop) who helps hotel patrons with luggage, transportation, and anything else that will make their stay at the hotel comfortable. The character takes great pride in his job, and his character always thanks everyone for coming to "his" hotel. If you need visualization, this movie should be streaming for you to watch, and I suggest paying attention to the hotel attendants and their attitudes. You want to hire staff with the same mindset.

When people are invested in their work, they show up early. Sometimes people don't own a car and take the bus to work. If someone is willing to take a bus to work, they're dedicated.

You've got to create a culture in which everyone feels they "own" a piece of the restaurant, and they want you to succeed as a matter of pride. I find that people like to have their own tables, and groups like to have a section that they call their own. This builds a sense of familiarity and ownership in your brand. The more pictures of your customers you put on the walls, the more frequently they will come back. When you find the right people to engage with these customers and other employees, you will have hired a dynamic staff.

Where Do You Find These Fantastic People?

So how do you find these incredible people? There are online classified ads and job search websites, and you might participate in job fairs and employment events. People who respond will tell you about their best qualities in glowing terms. Listen to your gut instinct. When you talk to someone on the phone or, better, meet with them, you know whether they're going to be a good fit or not. Remember, you are casting a role.

When you are hiring restaurant staff, you are going to be bombarded by employment agencies. These agencies will charge you about 20% of the salary of the hired employee. I understand the value of agencies doing the vetting and marketing to find great people; however, at this point the cost is too high, and you need your cash.

The best and most dedicated employees I've ever had in my restaurants, in my experience, came from Goodwill Industries. This organization offers programs to train people and help them get their necessary licensing to work in the food and beverage industry. Many times, Goodwill will pay for the uniform if the employee has to provide one. I find that the people who work through Goodwill are very motivated and have become some of our best staff members.

I encourage you to read books about hiring and staffing. Here is where guidance from others can help to build the right staff. It is not about creating a softball team in the off hours but hiring people who want to be of service. You want to hire people who are on the same page and understand the culture, and they should want you and everyone else to thrive and succeed through their personal efforts. I always look for people who have good problem-solving skills, with great attention to detail and time management skills. Remember that your wait staff are your salespeople and should have a level of interpersonal skills including social perceptiveness, patience, and empathy. This will all add to a better customer experience. Your wait staff needs to be active listeners with great communication skills. Lifting trays and standing on their feet all day requires the physical ability to do the job. And please don't forget math skills.

However, keep your ego out of it. If you're opening a restaurant, you are probably an alpha person. You need other alpha people to run a successful restaurant. I've learned to be able to yield my alpha personality and decide if it is beneficial to hire this type of person. Alpha people really want to be winners and will not allow for failure, and these are the people you need on the team. It is up to you to determine whether they will work with you and if you can control both of your egos. You and the alpha people need to understand that it is to both of your benefits if the restaurant succeeds, and that each of you can yield and be of service to each other, the staff, the vendors, and the customers.

Hiring the Stars of the Show: Chefs, Cooks, and Managers

One of the main staff people to be hired is the chef or chef de cuisine. You may already have that person, and all of the staff hired will have to work with your chef as a team.

More importantly, you need to know the levels of experience of the people you hire to be your executive chef, general manager, and/or lead cook. Do they know the rules and regulations of the required health cards? Different states call these cards by different names, such as *food handler card*, *food worker permit*, or *food handler certificate*. Health cards are always required for anyone who works in a food establishment, including kitchen staff, servers, managers, and anyone who could come into contact with food, ice, beverages, and utensils. Many jurisdictions are changing the rules to mandate that all food handlers be required to get a food handler safety-training card instead of a health card. To obtain a food handler's card, participants must take a food safety training course and pass an examination from an accredited organization. However, it is still your responsibility to ensure that your staff has complied with the health department and other government agencies.

You might not need an executive chef, but then you will need a lead cook. You personally might fulfill the role of a general manager, or you may have to hire a general manager. It's called *general* for a reason: you're overseeing everything, including the back of the house and the front of the house.

Your chef, general manager, and/or lead cook will tell you what staff they need in the kitchen. This could include dishwashers, expediters, chef de cuisine, salad makers, and sauce makers. They're going to give you their wish list.

Remember, this is just their wish list. You don't have to hire all those people just because the chef wants them. You don't need to create and fill those positions. I didn't hire chefs to work in my hamburger places. I had chef friends help and guide me. I hired cooks, and then my chef friends taught them how to cook the burgers as well as how to prepare the French fries and toss them. Of course, I showed them how to make my chili recipe.

Most modern kitchen teams today are based on a French chef's kitchen brigade system. Chef Georges-Auguste Escoffier was commonly known as "the king of chefs and the chef of kings." Escoffier's legacy lives on in the "brigade de cuisine" system. Having served in the French army, Escoffier transferred his experience with the clearly defined structure and duties of a military brigade into the kitchen, assigning over 20 specific cook positions throughout the kitchen. The purpose of the kitchen brigade was to ensure that every cook had a clear purpose and the kitchen could work to maximum efficiency. This system is obviously for a much larger restaurant but can be downsized for basic needs.

With that knowledge, you can see how you may need more than one cook, depending upon the concept, food style, and price point of the restaurant. A general rule of restaurant thumb is 6 to 7 back-of-house staff per 50 customers. If you have hired the correct lead cook or executive chef, that person should have the knowledge about what back-of-house staff are needed for your hours of operation. For additional staff, I have always found that you can reach out to trade schools, culinary schools, and college students. One important rule is that it has to be an accredited school. If there is an internship available, inquire about the requirements. Some states require that interns be paid, while other states allow for unpaid internships. Most schools do require students to participate and complete an internship program as part of their graduation requirements. Remember, these students are just learning to cook and are not experienced. However, they want to enter the culinary field and are motivated to become the best cooks possible, with many looking toward the future working as a chef.

Front-of-house wait staff should generally include a server for every three to four tables per shift per 50 customers as a good ratio. Remember that in addition to the wait staff, you may also need bussers, cleaners, greeters, and possibly a cashier. Study your budget, and you can determine any positions you can pick up to save the salary, or whether the wait staff can also greet and take care of the cashier position.

Do I Really Need to Touch That?

Everybody hired must be willing to "touch the table." What this means is that everybody fills the water glasses and clears plates. This is the kind of engagement that is required for success. You need to hire servers who, while serving their own tables, see that a teammate's table is full of dirty dishes and voluntarily clear the table. Anyone you hire who does not do that on their own as part of the team will hinder your success.

Everyone needs to work in unity. This is not about ego. This is about being of service. Don't hire people who won't perform other duties because they think they are too good or too special. I don't care how well a server can sell a meal. It will drive customers away if they are sitting at a table with no drinks or dirty dishes and they feel ignored. These patrons will notice if there are servers walking around and nobody notices that they are sitting at their table with no water in the glass. Every server should fill those water glasses regardless of whether it is their table.

Customers can see if a server is servicing someone else's table, walks by their table, and doesn't ask if the customers need anything. They know if someone is walking about with a coffee pot and doesn't come by their table to fill their cups. This changes the entire dining experience and does not build up loyalty, no matter how much the patrons might like the food.

I hire people with the understanding that no job is too low for anybody, including the greeter. Everybody has to help everyone else, and more importantly, wants to help everyone on the team. If you as the owner are willing to wash dishes and scrub the floors, then everyone hired to work there should be willing to perform the same duties as well.

Did I Just Hear a "No" from Someone I Want to Hire?

Yes, you will make some mistakes when it comes to hiring people. However, if you offer a job and someone turns you down, *do not assume* it was because of you and the restaurant.

This is neither the time nor the place to make assumptions and take anything personally. While you might think they are a perfect fit, the potential job candidate might feel differently. What if it is difficult for them to commute to your place? What if they were offered another job at the same time that paid more or had better benefits? What if they are struggling with addiction and decide to work in a place that does not sell alcohol? What if they are just uncomfortable with the culture and need to find one that fits them better?

If they don't accept the job, it's okay. It's all good and not a personal thing. I always tell potential staff members who don't accept a job offer to please give me a call if they change their mind. Remember, I liked them enough to offer them a job. You should feel the same way.

You should not dislike someone because they did not accept a job offer. What kind of a person does that? That's an ego thing, and it can hurt your success.

The food and beverage industry is like a roller coaster ride. People working in the industry are up and down and moving from place to place. Sometimes they never work for you. Sometimes they work for you, then leave, and never return. Sometimes people work for you, leave, and then come back. I welcome these people with open arms, and you should as well.

Training Your Staff

After hiring, it is time to train the staff properly to be a cohesive team. You should already have taken out your yellow pad or digital device and made a list of all the tasks. Try to be as complete as possible, since you are paying the staff to train, so squeeze a lot into a short time. Also, this will aid in writing an employee manual, which should be completed soon.

When hiring the new employees, including the restaurant managers and the cooks, you want to hire people with at least a few years of experience so you don't have to spend too much time training. They should be ready to fill the position effectively after the training period.

The first step in employee training is always orientation. This helps employees become familiarized with your restaurant and learn your best practices, facility, history, and culture.

When training, remember to always state the positive instead of the negative. It is better to say, "We serve butter already sliced," instead of "Never bring unsliced butter to the table." This will lend itself to a more positive experience for everyone.

Some of the tasks you should include for the front of the house are as follows:

- Training your greeters on proper ways to greet guests, monitor table rotation, take reservations, and escort guests to tables. All of this is to prepare the guest with a great start to their meal.

- Bussing tables: how to remove dirty items, what a table setup needs, and how to make sure diners aren't left without silverware, napkins, or condiments

- Taking orders: instructions on how to take orders, how to upsell, and how to use the POS system if one will be used or submit an order if another method is used.

- Menu knowledge: learning which dishes the customer could have allergies to, item substitutes, food preparation details, and which dishes are vegetarian, vegan, kosher, or gluten-free.

- Drink pairings: If you are serving wine or spirits, what wine or cocktail pairs with each dish and why the chef made that suggestion. If no beer, wine, or spirits will be served, what brand of soda, ice tea flavors, and other beverages are offered.

- Training on the proper way to run the food and carry food trays to and from the tables, how to serve hot food without getting burned, how to properly dispense wine and other beverages.

- Instructions on how to close out a ticket on the POS system and how to handle money and credit card payments. You should have decided what you are going to use for POS.

- Then, of course, the lessons you learned while hiring: using their interpersonal skills, such as dealing with demanding customers, problem-solving, and handling complaints.

Some of the tasks you should include for the back of the house are as follows:

- Walk through all the tasks needed in the kitchen.
- Teach your cooking preparations and process for each menu item.
- Walk through your expediting process with the wait staff.
- Give detailed instructions on how to operate the kitchen equipment safely, including grills, ovens, and dishwashers. Your cooks and chef will already know most of this information and can help develop a plan with you. But foremost is safety and accident prevention, especially from burns and knife injuries.

Speaking of Taste

Some of the most fabulous restaurants I know implement an excellent training program for the servers when it comes to setup, order taking, and serving the actual meal. However, many of them don't include tasting the menu, which is just as important as other aspects of working in the restaurant.

All of the staff (partners) need to be educated on the menu, try the various items, and really understand what your food is all about with its history, flavor profiles, concept, and mission. A staff member who doesn't know the menu and flavors is like an actor who doesn't know his lines. It leaves a bad taste (pun intended) in the patron's mouth.

How was the restaurant founded? Who is the owner? Why did they open the restaurant? What's in the food? Why is this dish on the menu?

For example, what if your restaurant started with an Italian sauce that comes from a 300-year-old recipe from the family of the owner's grandmother? The sauce that the restaurateur tops on the pasta has a history. Your staff needs to know this to tell the customers so they will want to try it.

Another example is fish and chips made with a recipe that came directly from the United Kingdom. Maybe the owner's great grand-mother used to go out, fish for cod, and make her own fermented beer as an ingredient for the batter.

If you, as the owner, have not invited the entire staff (including greeters, bus people, and dishwashers) for a day of tasting, that is a big mistake on your part. You need to have the staff taste every single dish and see how it is plated. You can serve family-style, putting two to three plates down for five people. But they need to know what they are selling by tasting it, and they should know the overall mission of the restaurant. They need to have the chef explain the dishes to them, including ingredients. Some of the most celebrated restaurants started with very few resources but still made sure the entire staff knew the menu by tasting everything so that they understood its concept.

Another mistake many owners make is hiring a staff member who will not try certain dishes. Of course, if there is an allergy or dietary restriction, I am not saying don't hire them. In fact, they will probably be more empathetic to customers dealing with allergies and restrictions. But if the server doesn't at least try something, that is not a person I would hire.

A good example is Brussels sprouts, those miniature cabbage-like vegetables. They are full of vitamins and minerals and have fiber, but I knew very few people who liked eating the vegetables, especially since they were usually prepared boiled and soaked in butter. One casino actually offered Brussels sprouts as a vegetable choice years ago, but only the diehard fans would order it.

Then something happened with this forgotten vegetable. Young chefs discovered it and became innovative with its preparation. Suddenly, Brussels sprouts were roasted, charred, and sautéed, becoming a new discovery with foodies.

You want to hire people who will at least try something new. They don't have to like it and eat it again, but those people who are willing to expand their palate and tastes make the best servers.

I have dined in restaurants and asked my server what their favorite dish is. If they answer that they haven't tried everything on the menu, the restaurant has just lost an excellent opportunity to create a returning customer. If a server has chosen not to try everything on the menu, and it is not due to allergies or dietary restrictions, you need to find someone else or plan to lose sales and customers.

How Can I Serve You?

There are a variety of ways to serve a meal, including hand-carried, tray, family-style, and cart service. I recall the stereotype of the waitress in a diner carrying six plates balanced on her arm. Some national chains with the diner vibe are still serving this way.

Remember, it is about your concept and what atmosphere you want to create with your restaurant. Whether it is a meal on the go, like my hamburger places, or a long European-style meal, it is part of the experience you are creating.

Delete the Word "Versus"!

It is not a competition between the front-of-house and back-of-house staff. Everyone needs to be on the same team, be of service, and work together. Everybody has to be on the same page.

I once witnessed a customer ordering a burger with blue cheese on it. The server put in the order, and the cook complained very loudly that it was too much work to add blue cheese to a burger. Yes, blue cheese is messy, the grill has to be cleaned after the order, and it is extra work. However, if blue cheese is available, the customer should be accommodated.

I have also witnessed a customer sending back a bowl of soup for being too salty. When the server brought back the soup, the chef swore and said there was nothing wrong with the soup, and why should he (the chef) be bothered for such a small order? The server was in the middle of the chef and customer, and it reflected on the environment of the restaurant.

Another instance I personally experienced was when I took my daughter to a restaurant that I love (including the owner and the food). The servers and cashier were busy, and one of the staff members from the back of the house cashed out our order. The cashier disagreed with the way the server wrote up an order and began complaining about this out loud in front of my daughter and me, as well as all the other customers and she made some negative comments. My daughter mentioned that she wasn't very nice, and no father wants that experience in a restaurant.

These are just three examples of what should not happen in your restaurant. If a server only orders a soup that retails for $5.95 and the customer complains about something, the size of the order should not matter. All customers should be treated like VIPs, with the mindset in your restaurant being that no order is too small. This should also be the attitude when customers order something special that can be accommodated. And no one should ever complain about another staff member in front of customers.

If your team doesn't function this way, it is a huge loss for you and your restaurant. This is a big part of the hiring process. Yes, skills, experience, and reliability are critical. But most importantly, you need a team that can work together and is engaged with each other to create a successful restaurant.

We all know that people make mistakes, have egos, and may lose their cool. There are a few simple steps to prevent this from creating any animosity to each other in the restaurant. When hiring and training staff, make sure everyone knows their role in the restaurant. When problems do arise, be sure the staff feels comfortable coming to you, and communicate effectively. You need to focus on the *why* rather than the *who*: that will decrease the blame. Enforce the fact that you are all on the same team, and make them accountable to each other.

Why Would Anyone Want to Leave Me?

I have witnessed many restaurant owners disassociate themselves from the staff and almost make themselves unapproachable. This is a wrong stance to take, since as we already discussed, your staff are a big part of creating the dining experience for your customers and are the face of your restaurant.

The biggest priority in your restaurant is that everyone needs to be on the same page. When you accomplish that, you will have a team that will make other business owners envious. You want people—including your competition—to say, "I want that person working for me." However, you need to be part of the equation for everyone to get along. Some people will be more dedicated than others at different times, and you need to understand that dynamic.

According to the National Restaurant Association, employee turnover across the entire restaurant industry is about 61%, and that percentage is almost twice as high for front-line workers. The shocking truth is that restaurants on average lose somewhere around $150,000 a year due to employee turnover alone. How can you make sure you are prepared for this? How do you avoid employee turnover? The answer is simple: hire right the first time.

Many things about that statistic are not under the control of restaurant owners. Let's focus on what you *can* control. Staff members always want more money and more hours. The lack of ability to make enough money in tips or other wages is a major reason employees leave jobs, especially in the restaurant industry. As we discussed, sometimes staff and management disagree. Other times, staff disagree among themselves. If this is not resolved, employees will quit. If a restaurant employee does not see an opportunity to advance, they are likely to leave. Most of these issues require periodic individual check-ins with your staff. If you can effectively plan with this in mind, you will decrease your restaurant's turnover rate.

There will be arguments among the staff, but do your best to keep them private and to a minimum. It is not about taking sides. It is about being of service; and you, as an owner, are of service to your employees just as much as your employees and your wait staff are of service to you and your patrons. It doesn't mean things aren't going on in people's lives, and life gets in the way. It's okay as long as you, as an owner, recognize that and remain the glue to keep everyone together.

In the End

When it comes to hiring the right people, analyze all the information and also listen to your gut (or intuition). Then make your decisions—because, in the end, it all circles into being of service. You have spent money to build this place. You have put your blood, sweat, and tears into opening this restaurant, and you are ready to create a place of partnerships, teamwork, and a chance for everyone to shine while customers enjoy a great meal. You know you have the most fantastic staff when a customer comes in and asks for a table for one because they are that comfortable.

It is all about repeat performances, long runs, and becoming a classic show (or in this case, a restaurant) where people will want to bring their children and grandchildren for years to come.

6 The Main Course

You've created this beautiful space, have all your tools in place, and you are now getting ready for the main course—the food. This is the next level of research, so grab that yellow legal pad, notebook, or device and get ready.

Always remember: when you make these choices, you are going to make some wrong decisions; but have faith and keep moving forward. Don't let misjudgments slow you down.

Meet with the chef or cook, and really go over your menu. Write down everything that's in every dish, from salt to racks of ribs to heads of lettuce, and how much you need of each item. You've taken photos of your ingredients, and you have ideas for how to present each dish. The one point you need to realize is that you only have one chance to make a first impression. You have dazzled your customers with your staff, the menu, and the atmosphere. Now comes the head-liner, so to speak: the food.

This Is Not a Trip to the Grocery Store

You need to meet with suppliers and vendors again to show them your menu, pictures, and list of ingredients. These account executives and vendors work the front line of the industry, meeting with restaurateurs daily. They know what food items are selling and what trends may have fallen flat. You can then look at the pricing and the cost structures. Suppliers and vendors will share information with you, but remember they are not your friends. Do not share all of your information with them or complain—that is only for your most trusted family members and friends. Keep it pleasant, and work on your orders. Stay transactional. I have become friends with many of our vendors in the past, and complaining about other vendors or products to them has only come back to bite me. The vendors have raised prices on me, knowing I had no other reliable resource to purchase a product or an ingredient.

Distributors such as Sysco (Sysco.com), US Foods (USFoods.com), Nicholas and Company (NicholasAndCo.com), and Chef Warehouse (ChefWarehouse.com), as well as food brokers in your city, will allow you to use their kitchens and prepare every item from your menu. They have chefs on staff who can develop recipes with you. Use this advantage. You will probably order the majority of your food from them, since these companies are the largest food distributors. If your city has a Restaurant Depot (RestaurantDepot.com), go in and introduce yourself and sign up for an account. I find that although they don't offer a lot of support, their products are excellent, and their prices are amazing.

If you want desserts such as ice cream, cakes, and pastries, these distributors offer them frozen. You can also purchase these items from Restaurant Depot, which will allow you to pick and choose your items right out of the warehouse. I like this option because it allows you to make choices on the spot to offer special items and unique desserts.

Sometimes distributors don't provide an item you'd really like to offer your customers, and you have to turn to Plan B. For example, I spent months looking for a birthday cake. Yes, a simple iced birthday cake that I could have cut into pieces and sell in my hamburger spots. This was one time that my creativity got the best of me. Who would have thought that you couldn't buy a simple birthday cake from a distributor? I had to turn to local wholesale bakeries to get what I needed, and it worked out wonderfully. They even ended up supplying us with less expensive hamburger buns. My research paid off.

Why did the local bakery offer me a lower-priced staple for my restaurant in conjunction with a supply of birthday cakes? They wanted that sale, and they wanted continuing orders. If you are successful, your distributors have a returning client with a thriving business. These companies have been in business for decades, and they know what works and what doesn't work.

Stay in the Home Court with Perishables

When you are ordering perishables, I recommend using a local vendor because they're already working on the shipping, and they're bringing in the units. Along with national distributors such as US Foods, Sysco, and Nicholas and Company, there are local distributors as well. The key is to get the food as fresh as you can at the least cost to you.

The food has to meet your requirements. What if something is wrong with the shipment of food? A local contact with whom you have developed a relationship will help you. If you ordered a case of tomatoes and 30 of them are bad, but you purchased them from a distributor three states away from you, you probably won't get any replacements, and you have to eat the cost of those bad tomatoes. Make a smart decision, and don't be penny-wise with fresh products.

Fresh Is More than Fruits and Vegetables

As much as you should love what you are doing, you are probably a little overwhelmed about both time and money. You are studying your menu and maybe thinking to yourself that you can save money and time using canned items.

I always advise using fresh whenever possible. Customers know the difference. I recently ordered wonton soup at a Chinese restaurant, and I knew they used a powdered broth. I can tell the difference, and I won't reorder it. Your customers appreciate fresh. However, you may need to use imported products such as canned European Italian tomatoes or jarred olives from Greece.

When you purchase canned or bottled prepared food items, make sure they are going to save you time, but don't compromise on flavor. While time is money, it can also cost less to make soups, sauces, dressings, dips, French fries, and other items from scratch, since buying the ingredients in bulk makes them less expensive per ounce.

Is Frozen Food Still Tasty?

Frozen food may save money, but make sure it never defrosted in transit. I've seen problems with frozen foods used at different restaurants. When purchasing patties of ground beef or cut up chicken, I found a lapse in the freezing, meaning the food was not frozen from processing to delivery.

For example, you can buy corn at the grocery store and open the package, and find that the corn is stuck together in a block of ice. This means the package of corn was defrosted and frozen again. Since the corn is going on your dinner table, you can return it and get another package. But when you are serving paying customers, you don't want a whole order defrosted and frozen again.

If you buy frozen, make sure it is flash-frozen, and order from vendors with an impeccable reputation. You can ask those in the hospitality industry as well as get recommendations from other chefs and restaurateurs.

Special Isn't Always Special

Don't get carried away with unique ingredients that are hard to find, or that only a few vendors carry.

I created a milkshake for one of our restaurants, and I used Fox's U-Bet chocolate syrup. I grew up with it on the east coast, and I loved it. I wanted to introduce it to the west coast, but nobody carried it. I couldn't find it anywhere but online. It was available in grocery stores, but I needed the commercial size.

The flavor was great, but if I didn't monitor the case lots coming in and out, we would sell out; and I couldn't switch to using another brand (remember consistency). This was added work—and since time is money, it was an additional cost to me. What I should have done, and am now advising you to do, was taste different chocolate sauces that were readily available to me and use the brand I liked best. The customers would have probably loved that milkshake as well. This time, I admit my ego was saying I needed to use only this chocolate syrup. I now know that I needed to source chocolate syrups. By the way, we did end up making the shake in other locations using a well-known brand, and it was a hit with the customers.

Living Off the Land

A big buzz term in the restaurant industry (since it is more than one word) is *farm-to-table*. Food is cooked from locally sourced ingredients, usually organic. While millennials might believe they created the farm-to-table trend, it has really been around since the late 1970s with the counter-culture movement (better known as hippies). The farm-to-table trend began with the development of member-based co-ops that made fresh produce and other natural food available to be purchased in areas outside of farming communities. In the 1980s, urban gardens were developed in the heart of many big cities. Home gardens followed, with tutorials on how to grow tomatoes and other plants in window boxes and on balconies.

What makes farm-to-table all-encompassing today is that the movement is now mainstream and part of our vernacular and dining experience.

If you want to source things locally, that doesn't mean going to the store and buying them locally. The term means the food has to be grown locally or comes from a farm. It is amazing what has become popular due to the farm-to-table trend. A great chef said to me that heirloom tomatoes used to be ugly tomatoes that were thrown away. The tomatoes were then given a fancy name, and now everybody wants them on the table.

Is this something you should be looking into for your restaurant? Well, it depends. If you want to have a very fancy place, be politically correct, and spend additional money, then you can consider adding farm-to-table items to your menu. If you are on a very tight budget, and you are offering, for example, burgers, you can add fresh tomatoes and other produce without spending a lot of money.

It does cost a little more to use farm-to-table food, including produce, meats, and other food items. You would think it shouldn't cost more because if it's local, there are no shipping charges, storage fees, up-charges, and distribution costs. But with additional farm taxes, the food becomes a little more expensive. I have always heard that it costs more to eat well. If you're going to spend more money to buy food, you have to charge more and make sure it is better.

If you promote your restaurant as local farm-to-table, make certain you only serve local farm-to-table ingredients. For example, let's say you run out of tomatoes, and you contact your local distributor to purchase more. Your customers believe your tomatoes are farmed locally, which means the tomatoes were grown and purchased from a local source. Yes, all tomatoes are grown on a vine with their roots in dirt (or hydroponically). However, if someone finds out you bought tomatoes grown 400 miles from your restaurant, crisis control can become your number-one priority if they make it known publicly. People take listing and promoting ingredients as local farm-to-table very seriously. One mistake involving perceived or real deception can destroy your reputation (and that of your restaurant).

You or someone from your team needs to physically visit the farms where you buy your locally sourced food. There is a great deal of scrutiny today, especially with restaurants, and you don't need any questions or complaints about serving food labeled locally sourced or farm-to-table when the food was transported long distance.

Rock 'n' Roll Chef Kerry Simon Did Farm-to-Table Right

One of the amazing things you can do as a restaurant owner is to change things like adding daily specials. I learned a lot from the late Chef Kerry Simon, who loved the earth, grew herbs, and worked magic in his kitchens. He sourced many ingredients and always made the right decision when it came to food.

Chef Kerry never put the words *farm-to-table* on any of his menus. But if he got in a shipment of pears, he would make a great pear salad, and it was on the menu until the pears ran out. He was fun that way. Doing this can add revenue to your restaurant since customers love new, limited-time items.

A Real Farm-to-Table Experience

A great way to increase your revenue is to change the menu and give the customers something unexpected. This also helps create repeat customers. A great example is a farm-to-table restaurant, Thomas Hill Organics Bistro & Wine Bar in Paso Robles, California. Everything is organic, and the experience is mind-boggling. Regular customers know that the menu changes to showcase the bounty grown on California's central coast. The restaurateur and chef also work with California purveyors to supply beef, lamb, poultry, fish, and game meat, and local artisans bake the loaves of bread. Some of their customers eat there three days a week.

Roofs and the Desert Become Green (Without Envy)

While urban gardens have been around for decades, with advanced technology, there is now urban commercial farming. Greenhouses are springing up in the desert, and urban farming has taken over rooftops in New York City. I think this is fun, and I want to support the movement.

But when you are just opening your restaurant and you have a budget, you would need to charge more for this food because it will cost more. If you plan to open a high-end restaurant, utilizing those resources will make a difference. But if you are opening a hamburger place and you want to use local urban farm–grown tomatoes from the rooftop of a building in Manhattan, be prepared. The tomatoes will probably cost three times more than from a distributor, and you will have to charge more for your hamburger. In this case, I advise against using the tomatoes because it may not be worth the price increase for success. However, if you really want to support this kind of farming, you can always negotiate by talking to the urban farmers and see what deal you can make. This would certainly be great for marketing and giving back to the community.

Isn't a Farmer's Market Locally Sourced?

The short answer is that you don't really know the answer. You could go to the local farmer's markets and source from there. But unless you visit the farm, how do you know what you're getting? You can go to a farmer's market and buy all of a vendor's apples and tomatoes. However, some of the vendors could have just purchased them from Sysco, US Foods, or a local produce wholesaler. I am not saying this is true of everybody who sells at a farmer's market, but you just don't know until you visit the farm.

A Well-Stocked Pantry

As for nonperishable food items, I like to source them from the internet and e-commerce vendors such as Amazon, eBay, and webrestaurant.com. These sites have saved me a lot of money. There are membership stores such as Sam's Club and Costco, as well as Smart & Final retail stores. I am a huge fan of Restaurant Depot. Amazon and eBay even offer a commercial division. Of course, you should have been doing research, so ordering your items is just finalizing your list.

While you can order dry and canned goods online, you have to be very careful to check the expiration dates. While e-commerce vendors monitor dates, you also need to watch the dates and check for damaged cans. Ultimately, it is your responsibility.

You also need to be very careful about authenticity. Maybe you love a great European tomato, San Marzano, and order it from an Italian distributor. First you need to check the seal on the container to be sure it comes from the European Union. Then you need to check the dates to make sure the tomatoes have not expired or will not expire in a short time. Of course, there is the expense of shipping and importing the product.

You need to be vigilant when it comes to canned products, especially from out of the country. An advantage of working with a local distributor is that there might be less expense involved, and they will work with you if something is wrong with the product.

Good Flavor Can Be Worth the Extra Expense

Many times you can use a canned product like tomatoes and create a wonderful flavor palate. Sometimes you want to spend a little bit more to get the right flavor because then people are going to buy more of your food.

A perfect example is an Italian restaurant I recently visited. The owner obviously spent a lot of money decorating the place, and it was beautifully laid out. We sat down, and a hot basket of bread was brought to our table. My mouth was watering from the aroma, and my eyes appreciated the beautiful presentation. Then our server poured the olive oil with balsamic vinegar, and I was ready to begin my meal. I carefully dipped the bread into the olive oil and balsamic and tasted it, and it was watery. I know balsamic.

This was my first time at the restaurant, and this was my first taste of the food. I knew a server who worked there, and I asked him what brand of balsamic they used. He responded that it came out of a big plastic jug. I knew it was a generic balsamic.

You might think I was too picky. But first impressions are crucial, and then the subconscious comes to the surface. I chastised myself for being petty (and I am in the industry), but my subconscious kicked in, and I realized I never wanted to eat there again.

The bread and olive oil were delicious, but this is a poor way to make a first impression with a first bite of food. If the owner had purchased a higher quality balsamic, it might have increased his cost by $5 per bottle. But that $5 would have ensured a great beginning to a wonderful meal, and the expense would be minimal compared to getting another loyal customer to add to that list of 3,000 paying customers I recommend for success. I could taste that the olive oil was good quality along with the fresh bread; but mixed with cheap balsamic, the owner missed that flavor profile by being penny wise and pound foolish.

Be Consistent with Every Dish Every Time

While I have made a case for using fresh whenever possible, now I will explain why you can use canned ingredients and remain consistent while serving great food.

Let's use as an example a restaurant that's open for breakfast. You and the chef want to make sausage gravy from scratch to serve on chicken fried steak and biscuits, even though it is not a family recipe. You create the right flavor with the right amount of sausage and spices, and the gravy is a hit. However, the chef, cook, or you really have to watch that pot of gravy on the stove because it can begin to burn, and when that happens, the whole batch is ruined.

After you burn it a few times, you discover you don't have enough ingredients to make more gravy. What if there is a big demand for a dish with your gravy? You can't switch to canned ingredients, because customers will be able to tell the difference. Customers then will not trust anything that is served and will find someplace else to eat. Do I need to remind you about reviews and posting on social media?

Now, if you start with a can and add seasoning, spices, and herbs, you can make the gravy taste amazing. Ask distributors and brokers for recommendations, try every single one so you know what flavor you want, and then mix it with your herbs, spices, and seasonings. If the brand you like best is a little more expensive, it is worth the cost. You can keep a supply of cases of the #10 cans, and you will never run out.

You can also use premade items such as ketchup and add your own ingredients like mustard seeds to make it uniquely your own. I saw this done a very high-end steak house, N9NE at the Palms Casino Resort, which was at the time the go-to spot for celebrities visiting Las Vegas. Chef Barry Dekake actually used a brand-name ketchup with added mustard seeds, served in a small ramekin with their hand-cut French fries. It was a brilliant display of adding value and flavor to a product used in many households.

Another big seller is marinara sauce. Unless this is the main ingredient of your recipe (like grandma used to make), vendors might offer premade marinara in a can; or, as I discussed, you can use canned Italian tomatoes instead of fresh tomatoes. Yes, it is more time-consuming to make your own sauce. Test it and see if you can save time and money buying canned tomatoes and then adding your own spices, such as garlic and basil. As a restaurant owner, you're not going to have the time to stew and jar tomatoes, and canned European tomatoes are delicious.

If it's a pizza place, you can doctor up your pizza sauce, which is less expensive than relying on fresh ingredients. I know a restaurant that adds a jar of grape jelly to a canned pizza sauce. At certain times of the year, fresh may cost less, but out of season, buying those fresh ingredients can be more expensive. Then what are you going to do? Switch to canned tomatoes? You can't, because you need to remain consistent and either use fresh or canned tomatoes.

Just open that can, and get going. But be consistent.

Never Leave Your Shelves Empty

Now is the time to purchase your first inventory of food. You will need the advice of your distributors and your chef, who should be able to break down your inventory. Talk to your staff, because they know what they have and what they need.

When you first open, you can't forecast the flow of the restaurant or the food and supplies you will need. Even though you may need to buy larger quantities of food at one time from your suppliers, you don't want to overbuy perishables, because that will lead to spoilage and waste food (along with your money). You don't want to throw away money in the form of rotten tomatoes. You also don't want to under-order, because you don't want to run out of food for your customers. It's a fine line, but the only way you will know is by practice—I mean when your restaurant is open, and you can finally understand its flow.

Here are some simple ways to avoid waste:

- Make sure you only purchase the ingredients that your restaurant uses.
- Always keep the refrigerators and freezers at the right temperatures. Temperature control is essential for food safety, as it will prevent the growth of bacteria.

- It is imperative to always have clean surfaces inside and out of refrigerators since cleanliness is vital for ensuring quality and preventing pathogenic bacterial growth.

- Rotate inventory regularly. A common rule in the restaurant business is the FIFO rule First In, First Out, when storing food and displaying food for sale. The newer stock is behind the older stock, enabling the older stock to be sold first.

- Always label your food correctly, especially if it is separated from the packaging for storage. Keep the labels clearly written with the date and name.

- Inventory is essential, so always know what you have in stock at all times. Keep a detailed list of the foods in storage, including their use-by/best-before dates.

- Always inspect your deliveries and make sure they include what you ordered. Only accept the items you ordered, and reject products with visible spoilage or damage that you will be unable to use.

- Don't do any large-batch cooking before you know the demand for the dish; the food may not be sold before it goes out of date.

- Use recipe leftovers efficiently. You might be able to make soup, croutons, or sandwiches.

- Train the staff on these ways to reduce food waste as well.

You can break down the cost per the number of meals you want to serve, with a goal of earning $3,000 each day the restaurant is open. This is where you will learn to break down each meal to see the pricing per plate, the amount of food on the plate, your cost, and how many meals you predict you will sell.

When I was operating a simple burger place, I ran out of hamburger buns. How the heck could I let that happen? We were overwhelmed with business and did not track our inventory properly, since it is only logical to have the same number of buns as hamburgers. This is what happens when you don't prepare, plan, and predict. Be prepared to be overwhelmed.

The restaurant rule of thumb is that food should be turned over four to six times per month. Don't freak out when you hear the word *inventory*. Managing your inventory is vital to your restaurant and your profits. Have your managers do inventory reports at least once per week. Remember that ordering control will also free your cash from being tied up in unnecessary inventory. There are many benefits to truly knowing what the heck you have in stock or what you may be missing. You can also have the same manager do the ordering with the vendors, but keep in mind that you are ultimately responsible.

There is also software available that can help simplify the inventory task and keep you on track at the same time. If you don't want to go to the expense of buying inventory software, and if your POS system does not track any inventory for you, I suggest that you go online, search for "restaurant inventory management," and download one of the many free templates that you can use.

Time to Start Rehearsing

Now you're going to create every single plate on your menu. What do the French fries, chicken barbecue dish, sandwich, and prime rib plates look like after they are created in your restaurant's kitchen?

Photograph each one and compare it to the photos you took of how you envisioned that dish. Work on it, and photograph it when that plated dish matches what you want to present to your customers. Then, list the ingredients and the recipe. There needs to be consistency with every chef and cook preparing that dish. You will have copies of the pictures hanging in the kitchen, along with the book of photos, ingredients, and recipes.

What if something happens with one of your purveyors, you can't get a specific ingredient, or something doesn't taste right? You want to change it immediately; and by preparing everything in advance, you know that the dish will still taste and look the way you envisioned.

How Much Is Too Much?

Here is a question to consider: how big should the portion sizes be that you serve?

When people decide to eat in a restaurant, those customers want value as well as great food. I believe that to be a good value, the food needs to be abundant. Sometimes abundance could just be a giant yeast roll, taking up half the plate and looking big and plentiful. It's not expensive for you, but it gives added value to your patrons. That's going to bring them back to your restaurant over and over again.

I always advise offering abundance when you're creating your menu. This doesn't mean losing money on meats and other high-price protein items. This means adding potatoes, vegetables, bread, rice, pasta, and other items that enhance the meal and fill up your customers.

Some ideas include cooking mashed potatoes with chunks of potatoes because while it fills the plate (and stomach), you're using fewer potatoes with cost savings.

An Example of Great Value

A friend of mine, Jim Reese, developed the Hard Rock Cafés with a team and many years later, spotted a winner, Hash House A Go Go, based in San Diego. Jim loved it so much that he took the concept national. People couldn't believe the quantity of food on their plates.

Let's break down the menu. The biscuits are double-sized, served with butter and honey; and because they taste so good, people start to get filled up on the biscuits. Then the food comes out with a huge sprig of rosemary standing in the middle of the plate as garnish. The plate is oversized, traditionally used as a serving tray, and filled with about 60% percent mashed potatoes. If chicken is ordered, the cooks pound it out so big that it crawls over the plate. If you happen to order a simple salad, it will come in a serving bowl most often used for catering large parties. While it is considered a moderately priced restaurant, people are full and take leftovers home; they are happy to get excellent value for their money. This equals lines out the door.

That's value, but that also comes back to the idea of your mission to open the restaurant. Details like abundance on the plate will drive people to return to your restaurant.

Your Cost Versus the Menu Price

Always consider the costs. For example, break down the cost for that piece of chicken. Customers don't want to pay an excessive amount of money for little value. This is where your chef or cook can help, because they know how to price food. But you need to make sure the cost of the food stays within a percentage of that plate. If you want to charge $10 a plate, to then make a profit, your cost for the food on that plate should not exceed $3. If you plate food that costs the customer $10 using $3 worth of food, but it looks like its value is $30, you understand the concept and are winning the game.

I doubt you would be reading this book if you wanted to open a nouveau riche place that presented a little morsel of food with beet juice swirled on a plate like a work of art and charged an obnoxious amount of money for that "plate." Of course, I have seen chefs with reputations and a big ego open that kind of restaurant, only for it to close down. But you are reading this book, so I am working with you on building success.

Use One Meal to Market the Next Meal

As you develop your menu with actual costs, you also need to prepare your marketing strategy. I know of many steak houses with half-priced specials on Sunday or Tuesday nights that are packed on those nights. This is part of the restaurateur's marketing strategy. But you want to engage people and have them return regularly. Start writing down innovative ideas based on the menu, beyond Happy Hour, early bird, and lunch menus. Always keep in mind that these specially priced menus are a way for customers to sample your goodness and spread the word for your benefit. You see this daily with Indian luncheon buffets. Have you ever wondered why Indian restaurants don't offer buffets for dinner? It is because they want customers to come in for lunch and try the different items, so they feel comfortable ordering off the regular menu when they come in for dinner.

Pour Me Another One

Selling beer, wine, and spirits is a totally different business. I know many places that make 60% of their revenue from the sales of alcoholic beverages. The sales of beer, wine, and spirits need to be focused on properly since it is a different business within your restaurant business, especially if you want to offer a full bar. I'm not saying don't do it, but it's also going to cost more to include beer, wine, and/or spirits.

Still, liquor sales are another way to make money and can be included in your plan to open a restaurant. There is a potential for loss, such as if the bartenders over-pour or under-pour a drink. If someone doesn't like their drink, it gets poured out, and that is a loss. There are mixers, staff, bar equipment, cocktail menus, and insurances, which include extra costs. If you just want to offer beer and wine, do you sell by the glass, or do you charge by the bottle? Additional attorney's fees, licensing, and permits are required. There is pricing to consider. It really is another business.

My advice is that you focus on opening your restaurant first and then consider adding beer, wine, and spirits once the restaurant business becomes successful. You are opening a restaurant because you understand food, whether you are a chef, an entrepreneur, or both. For example, if you are opening a hamburger place, you know how to combine hamburger, lettuce, tomato, ketchup, sauce, and bun. You understand about the labor that it takes to make it, the plate to carry it out on, and the cost of the food. Focus on the restaurant, and in the future you can always add alcoholic beverages.

Dress Rehearsal

Finally, your kitchen and front of the house are complete, you have trained your staff, and everyone on the team has prepared and tasted the food and drink. Now is the time for a full dress rehearsal, just like in the theater. This is your production.

Plan a "friends and family night" so people can order off the menu and you can see how the restaurant will operate. These nights are fun for everyone who has shared your dream, even if you just talked to them about it. Dress rehearsals are always entertaining because you've already cast your entire theater. Think of "friends and family night" as attending a child's play in sixth grade.

You don't charge anyone for the food. I know some restaurateurs who work with charities to accept donations on those days. Offer everyone a chance to order off either the entire menu or a limited menu. Tell them to be patient, because your kitchen staff may not be up to speed at that point. There will be expenses for food, and you do need to pay the team. You want to do the best you can with food, service, and atmosphere. Once your friends and family leave, even though it's a dress rehearsal, they are going to tell people about your restaurant, and you don't want any negative reviews.

This soft opening is essential to determine how your kitchen flows without it being open to the public. You can correct any hiccups, receive valuable input, and see your team in action.

Are you ready to open a restaurant?

7 Learn From Reviews and Opinions

You have unlocked the door, turned on the lights, prepared your team, and you have a full supply of food. You have opened your restaurant, and you can barely contain your excitement to tell the world so customers can join you in your new restaurant. You just *know* you will get great reviews, so you want to invite the press, food critics, and Yelp Elite right now as well as start your advertising and marketing.

Stop! Don't get trigger happy!

There are still things you need to work through before you have a horde of people walking through your door to eat. No matter how wonderful it would be to be sold out every night with every table full, you don't want that to happen yet. This is part of the process of working out all the kinks. You need to embrace the trickle of customers so you can continue to work at your restaurant to make it and keep it successful.

You must now ask everyone's *honest* opinion. This is why you need to reach out to everyone you know, even if they attended "friends and family night," and get their opinion about the restaurant after the very quiet soft opening. You need to read the reviews that will pop up and speak with customers. Listen, just don't hear what they say, and write it all down.

You have your social media pages up, and you've launched your profiles on review pages. You are going to be bombarded with opinions and advice. Take a step back, catch your breath, and get ready for one of the most intense steps.

You need to navigate other people's opinions, especially criticism, know how to handle it, and make it work for you to really bring your restaurant up to the next level.

The "F" Word

As the founder of *Food & Beverage Magazine*, I really understand the effect that critics, reviews, and buzz can have on the success of a restaurant. From the professional critic to the average backseat restaurateur, you need to listen and use their opinions as a chance to improve. Long ago I learned about successes and failures from talking to many people.

Yes, the "F" word—*failure*.

The reason I'm writing this book is that I know what I learned from my failures, and I quickly learned that success doesn't teach us as much. Sometimes we don't know how or why something worked, or why something didn't. You have to give credit to some luck with the planning. Other times, you can only see what failed after it happened.

I have had some big failures for sure. While this example is not restaurant-related, it is just as relevant. When I was working in the floral business, my ego took over, and I leased locations from failed flower shops thinking that I had the "it" factor that could make it work. Well, looking back, it didn't matter what I had. These were just bad locations that cost my team and me lots of hard-earned money and time trying to make them successful. I should have simply focused on what was already successful, instead. Did I really need a huge box truck when the vans were delivering everything just fine? No: it cost us a fortune because the truck would not fit into parking garage delivery entrances, battering the fiberglass roofs. If it ain't broke, don't fix it!

We have all witnessed restaurants that open multiple locations without planning properly, just to close a few months later. There are the epic restaurant fails that I have watched, and some I have even tried to stop. One of them was a fried chicken fast casual restaurant concept in a Vegas outdoor shopping center by high-end restaurateurs selling a chicken breast priced over $5 with no sides in the 110-degree summer heat.

Don't Take It Personally

This is your livelihood, your dream come true, and your passion. However, you have to take everything told to you in the right light. People are talking about your food, not your family. They will love it, criticize something, or hate everything. They will "advise" you to add items, change the recipe, do this, and don't do that, and they will point out more than you can ever imagine. You must make sure you listen to opinions and write them down—but don't implement anything new yet.

I've seen restaurants adjust something because someone told them that it should be changed. For example, someone might say to the owner that instead of cooking French fries one way, it should be done another way. The next day, the restaurant changes how they cook their French fries. Why? One person told them to change it. Don't do that.

Once we sold the hamburger restaurants to a new restaurateur, and people told him that he needed to add nachos. I tried to tell him that this was not a Mexican restaurant, and he didn't need to add nachos. Well, he added nachos to the menu. Then he added chicken wings because someone else suggested it. Every time somebody suggested something, he would add it to the menu. Do you know what happened? He went out of business because he wasn't true to himself and the vision, which was owning a fun hamburger place.

Make a Note of What Customers Like

Many restaurants place cards on the table for people to rate the restaurant and write their opinion. But the reality is that they're going to tell you instead of writing it.

Recently my family ate at a great Italian restaurant, Roma II. I had to tell Fausto, the owner, that I love his pasta, my wife (who was a baker) loves his pasta, and the kids love his pasta.

I know where I can get a good bottled Alfredo sauce and Fra Diavolo, but I can't buy his pasta in the grocery store. This is why we return as customers. He told me he makes it fresh every day, and that is one of his secrets to his success.

I don't know him and how he operates, but I would advise him to write down my comment in a book with all of the other comments he receives. If he had asked me my name, I would have told him that I am Michael Politz, publisher of *Food & Beverage Magazine*. Then he really should have made a mental note and written down that the publisher of *Food & Beverage Magazine* loves the pasta. This should be in his notes, so if more people comment on the pasta—and I would imagine those comments would be positive—he knows to continue to make it fresh.

Yes, people will tell you positive things as well as negative. Remember to write everything down and think about it. However, don't let one person influence you to make a significant change.

Embracing 1- to 5-Star Ratings

Let's start with those 5-star reviews. Your friends and family are going to pump you up, especially if they think they will get free food when they go to your restaurant. They might have tried to dissuade you or talk you out of opening a restaurant, but now that it is a reality, they not only want you to be successful but also want to be the reason for your success.

Then there are those 1- or 2-star reviews, maybe from your competitors, people you chose not to hire, and customers. Unfortunately, a lot of competitors have their employees post against other places. You still must read the reviews and be ready! There will be reviews from customers who either didn't like something about the meal or had a problem with service. If somebody writes a negative review, you can reach out to them and ask them to come back in. If they give you a great review, then you can thank them with a free appetizer or dessert on their next visit. That will make their next visit sooner.

It is critical, though, to embrace everything, positive and negative.

Everybody wants to be successful. When you have to read a negative review, don't take it to heart, and don't take it personally. However, if the same criticism comes up again and again, it is certainly time for you as the owner to fix the issue. Are multiple customers complaining about the meat being too rare or overcooked? Get on the grill with the cooks, and fix the problem. Are people complaining that the chicken is too dry or the vegetables are overcooked? Then fix it. One complaint is too many complaints; but if you get two, then there may be a grain of truth in what the customer is saying. Take action immediately. Don't re-create your menu or go into some sort of down-the-rabbit-hole tailspin; simply fix the issues. Remember, you want to give and be of service to everyone. You are doing fantastic things, and your work is consistent, so remember: do not take any of this personally. Keep that top of your mind while reading reviews, to take the sting out.

What if the reviews are off the charts on all the different review sites? People are reading and talking about the reviews. But you also need to read those reviews with a grain of salt and not let them go to your head. You still need to be of service and work hard to become successful and remain successful.

The Power of Turning a Negative Around

Remember that everyone has different likes and dislikes as well as different expectations. Some will criticize if the taste is bland to them, they may compare the pasta to SpaghettiOs, or maybe they don't like the butter cold. Any of these negative personal experiences can show up in an online review. Some people writing these reviews don't even realize that they are giving a poor review. And many people don't understand that a bad review can be very detrimental to the owner, chef, and staff and their families. You as the owner must deal with this issue immediately. Again, this is a fine line, and you always need to find a way to turn a negative into a positive.

The more consistent you are, the less chance that a problem behind the scenes (including someone's bad day) will ruin a customer's dining experience. For example, if something spoiled came in from a vendor, throw it away and take it off the menu (or tell the customers it is not available that day); that is one problem you can avoid. In Chapter 5, I wrote that if the staff is invested in the success of the restaurant, they can quickly take care of any problem. These steps will help to mitigate many bad experiences. If a customer complains while dining, you must—and I mean *must*—attend to the issue immediately. This will turn any bad comments into positive ones. They may say they had an issue, but they will also say you handled it like a champion, and you will get a shining review.

The owner of a small Italian restaurant told the story of how a customer complained that the tomato sauce was "not red enough." Instead of rolling his eyes, the owner took the time to speak with the customer and found out their concerns. It turns out they believed that canned sauce was used and not fresh tomatoes. This particular restaurant did make their sauce from scratch, so the owner took the customers on a tour of the kitchen to show them. It took time and effort, but it was worth it. There was no bad review, and he probably cultivated these customers (and their friends and family) for life. This is why you write all comments down and why you interact with everyone.

There Are Times You Should Ask for Help

Of course, when people criticize, you will listen and decide if it is something for you to change or if someone is being overly critical.

If the same dish has numerous issues that need to be addressed, find another restaurateur who can give you some advice, and don't be afraid to ask for this help. If there is someone in the industry whom you admire, you can write to them or call and ask for advice in such a way that you're not bugging them. And it's incredible how, when you reach out to people, they want to help. Once you start receiving advice, please respect people and their time and really listen, take detailed notes, study them, and decide what changes you need to make based on the knowledge of those you respect. My advice is that when you ask for suggestions, you need to follow them. Nothing is more obnoxious to me then when people ask for advice and then do the opposite and fail.

Only Good Things to Say

When I created *Food & Beverage Magazine*, I had the chance to talk to great chefs like Wolfgang Puck, Bobby Flay, David Burke, Piero Selvaggio, Paul Prudhomme, and Kerry Simon. I would speak to them separately, and we would engage in the hospitality industry. I had a great opportunity to learn from them, and I am sharing those insights with you.

In 20 years of publishing *Food & Beverage Magazine*, we've never criticized anyone. This is why we don't do reviews. We only want to report the positive. While many others don't share our philosophy, many do. Bad reviews are painful, and criticism is harsh, but keeping a positive attitude, no matter what feedback you are receiving, will always make your restaurant that much better. Customers love to see restaurants take action on any feedback, and they feel honored to be the catalyst of that action.

Don't Believe the Hype

Here is a scenario: you are getting rave reviews and taking care of any negative ones, and everyone is urging you to push the word out and get media and food critics to come try your food.

You are thinking, "I can't fail. The reviews are all good, everyone loves my food, and I am the greatest."

That is the path to failure.

I witnessed this lesson personally with my friend Mike Tyson, who was once called the greatest boxer in the world. His fans would say, "He's going to kill everyone in the ring; he's going beat everyone." Mike received accolades from the media and fans constantly.

Mike didn't believe the hype at first. He knew he still had to train and work hard. He used to wear a jacket that said, "Don't Believe the Hype."

However, Mike made a detour on the road of life. His entire world shifted. He wrote in his autobiography that he started to believe the hype from everyone that he was the greatest boxer, and his brain told him he didn't need to go to bed early or train as hard as he could before a fight. He admitted that it was a big mistake, and now he goes to bed early, works hard, and operates a big corporation. He might not own a restaurant, but the concept is still the same. When you get great reviews and accolades, please stay humble. Always maintain the work ethic that you have now. Do not take one customer for granted; and know that a full restaurant and great reviews are amazing, but that doesn't mean you can rest now.

The Chef Who Set the Bar on Class

Chef Kerry Simon was one of my greatest mentors. We talked almost every day for over 20 years until his passing. He was handsome, charming, charismatic, and known as the rock 'n' roll chef. He became friends with every rock star and movie star you could imagine. I saw female movie and rock stars fall at his feet, and his attitude was, "Let me help you up and give you some of my food."

He never believed any of the hype, and he became more and more successful. Kerry wasn't a great TV star chef because that is not what he wanted. He always worked harder and created more dishes, built brands, and grew his restaurants. He also loved it when rockers like Quiet Riot's Kevin DuBrow, Justin Timberlake, and Robin Zander and Rick Nielsen from Cheap Trick ate in his restaurant.

Kerry would travel with Lenny Kravitz or Vince Neil of Motley Crue to help cook for the guys traveling on the road. He wasn't getting paid; Kerry just did it because he loved it. His love of the industry and his creativity opened up a whole other world for him, which was terrific. Kerry was the most unassuming human being you've ever met. He was very Zen, and I can share now that his password was always *bluezen*.

Kerry commanded the Edwardian Room at The Plaza. He was the chef there; celebrities joined the round table of people, and everyone had a great time. In his restaurants, nobody ever stayed at their table. People worked the room, and it was a crazy group, including musicians like David Lee Roth, Taylor Dane, Matchbox 20, U2, and the Rolling Stones. You never knew who would be in his restaurant.

When all these people were in his restaurants, do you think Kerry was hanging out with them? No. He was in the kitchen cooking, and he very rarely came out.

Kerry loved to cook, and he worked hard; that is how he rolled. He wanted to get the food perfect, and that is how he developed his reputation. He was happy to be doing what he was doing without all the accolades. He never ate dinner until well after dinner service was over; usually you could find him sitting at his bar talking to his staff around 11:00 p.m., eating his dinner. He softly held court, going over the night's events. He had the perfect attitude, and this is a good one for you to cultivate, fitting it to your personality.

Time for You to Shine

In the next chapter, you will get ready for the *big* opening when you invite all your friends, the media, and the general public so you can dazzle them with your food.

The curtain is ready to go up, and it will be opening night for you.

8 Getting the Word Out that You're Open for Business

You have now been open for business for at least two or three weeks since your soft opening, you have stopped panicking and are able to breathe. Money should be coming in and, hopefully, you're almost breaking even on a daily basis by this point. You're not going to be able to start paying back the opening expenses yet, and you may still have slow days, so be prepared, and don't freak out. The operation of the restaurant should certainly be going more smoothly. You will now collect data on your customers, and you are keeping to-do lists for the restaurant. Once you feel comfortable, you can plan for the grand opening and really put your marketing into action.

Every person you meet can become one of the 3,000 people you need in your database to make your business succeed. These are customers, not just people who know your restaurant exists. You need 3,000 people who have walked in and spent a dollar or more in your place. Marketing, public relations, and advertising dollars will keep those numbers moving upward, and that's what this chapter is all about.

The Big Reveal: Who Should You Invite to Your Restaurant?

The short answer is to invite everyone you know to your grand opening, along with their friends and friends of friends.

The long answer is the same, but you should have compiled a list with data about your customers, and now you will need to make that list even longer with potential customers.

As you know, I love to write lists, and I use yellow legal pads all the time. In previous chapters, I encouraged you to write things down instead of using digital devices.

This one is different. Start looking into customer relations management software designed for restaurant use. Hopefully you (or someone who can help you) know Excel or other spreadsheet software. Create a spreadsheet with headings such as name, email address, phone number, address (if possible), birthday, anniversary, social media names (handles), how you are connected, mutual contacts, and special notes such as allergies or favorite dishes. You can also do this in a Word document. I do recommend doing this digitally since people's information continually changes. This information will become vital to your marketing. The more information and data you have on your customers, the more ways you can attract them to come back in. Remember, you need a customer base of 3,000 people.

Let's break down the list. You will be amazed at the number of people you know and can invite to try your restaurant.

Family First

Of course, you know your immediate family, and you will want to include them on your list. But here is where you will discover the six degrees of separation to meet and add new people.

For example, you list all of your first cousins, spouses, and children who live in your city. If your cousins' children are married, what about their spouses? They have friends, co-workers, staff, and neighbors. Then you will want to include those connections. While you will want to do this with all of your relatives who live in your city, you will not be able to create the entire list at once. But this is a beginning, and you have to start somewhere. You will be surprised how quickly this list will grow.

Your Professional Life

Next, think about your professional life and break it down. Before you opened a restaurant, did you have co-workers, staff, supervisors, and/or a big boss? Write them down individually, and then you can expand on each name.

Here is where social media will be a useful tool. Before you say "cyberstalking," know that everyone looks at everyone else's social media. There is nothing wrong with looking up names on Facebook, Instagram, and LinkedIn.

You can read whether someone still lives in the same city and what they are doing now. You can see if you have anybody in common with connections or Facebook friends or followers. Social media is another way to reach out to people, especially if you have lost touch. There is nothing wrong or creepy about inviting someone to try your new restaurant. They can always ignore your invitation. This is a great way to both reconnect and fill your list with important data and contacts.

Who Else Do You Know?

Think about high school and college. If you joined a fraternity or sorority, whom can you reach out to now? What about former mentors? People you know from your place of worship can be added to your list. If you have volunteered, there are those people you can add to the list. There are political contacts and affiliations. What about a former spouse or boyfriend or girlfriend (if you are on good terms)?

You probably don't even know the number of people who know you, and you'll discover how far your reach is in the world. Now's the time to reach out and invite them to try your new restaurant.

The (Business) Cards Are Stacked with You

Since being an entrepreneur is in your blood, I am sure you have been collecting business cards along the way. Now they can finally come in handy!

There are apps and software to scan in business cards directly to a spreadsheet. Of course, the business card will not include where you met and other personal stats such as marital status and birthdays. But it is a start.

Many restaurants use a simple marketing tool to build up a database: a big bowl with a sign that says to drop in a business card to win a free lunch. This might be a first-time customer who loves the idea of winning a free lunch. Of course, some won't drop in a card, but always be friendly and invite them back.

Always try to get a business card for your database. If the chance to win a free meal doesn't do it, have the server ask for one. The key is to always be building your database.

If you're using technology as your point of sale, you can ask for an email to send the receipt. The more information you're capturing, the easier it is for you to get them back into your door. I have also seen many restaurants place cards on the table to ask customers if they want to be added to the mailing list.

Reach Out Digitally

As you are collecting this vital customer information, you will need tools to engage people. I create engaging opportunities each time I reach out. I have created newsletters, special offers, and special invites that I use to blast out to the database. You will need to use a non-transactional email service such as MailChimp (mailchimp.com), Mad Mimi (madmimi.com), or Constant Contact (constantcontact .com). There are many advantages to using these services; the main reason is that your personal email account will not allow you to send out thousands of emails in a flash. Also, someone can complain to the email service if they believe they are receiving spam from you. A non-transactional email service gives people a choice to opt out if they don't want to receive the blast for whatever reason, and they will be immediately removed from your database. Don't take it personally if someone opts out; it is not about you.

Putting Your Restaurant's Name Out There through Social Media and the Media

You are ready to tell the world that the restaurant is open. Now you need to figure out how to bring in customers outside of your database. Do you hire a public relations firm or social media guru? Do you hire an advertising agency? Can you reach out to the media yourself?

In previous chapters, before you made any decisions, you had to do research. In this chapter, before you make any decisions, keep reading. After reading the chapter, you will have the information you need to make an informed decision.

The First Step

While print (including magazines and websites), television, and radio are still around, the number-one communicator today is social media. This somehow became my field of expertise (marketing). Using social media effectively, you should have lines of people waiting to eat your food. This is a big endeavor. If you have the budget, you can hire a company or a person to handle your social media. But for those of you with a $25,000 budget, you can do this yourself. You just need to find the time.

As you collect everyone's information, your social media sites should slowly start to be populated as you gain diners and invite people to follow your restaurant's social media accounts. Try to be consistent about how often you post images and other information such as specials. I would recommend daily; but right now, if that is too much, at least pick a day and maintain that schedule. It is vital to keep your social media sites current.

Maybe someone on your staff loves social media and will want to help you. But give them direction to stay on brand, and always read the postings. Remember, it is your restaurant, and social media represents you and the restaurant.

Talk to your food vendors, because they can offer special food images and events you can post. If you have special new menu items, people want to know; so put them on social media, and make sure you include a hashtag. However, keep it evergreen. Remember, any specials you post with a discounted price will stay on your timeline forever, and people will pull up the post on their phone. If you are offering a half-price special on Monday, be prepared for someone to pull up that post a year after you posted it.

When you get a good review, share it, screenshot it, and post it on social media, and be sure to thank the person. You already have your photos, so start posting those pictures.

Remember, people engage with people. If they start talking to you on a social media site, respond to them. If someone posts something positive, be certain to thank them and maybe offer a free beverage the next time they come in and show the post.

How Do You Handle Negative Posts?

Engage the person who wrote the post. Sometimes you will need to apologize. Sometimes you can use humor. I engage people in different ways based on different concepts. The hamburger concept

I developed for my restaurants was snarky, implying it was a low-end hamburger, and what did you expect? We answered in more of a comical tone, and it became a lot of fun for the staff to help come up with responses. Then people would share those crazy responses with friends. It ended up giving us more business.

Someone would post, "I waited an hour." My response to them on social media would be, "You're lucky you didn't wait two hours." Another favorite of mine is, "I don't like onions, but my burgers had onions." My response would be, "Why are you crying over onions? You're not the first person to cry over onions."

You don't want to be too obnoxious, but if you can pull it off, people will respond by telling you, "I couldn't wait to read your posts."

If you feel you can't pull that off with humor, then respond with, "Come on back in, and we'll take care of it." But always respond and engage.

You don't want to become too personal, and always keep it above board. If you promise something, deliver.

Remember to use hashtags—and by the way, you can invent hashtags. Promote using the hashtag, keep it consistent, and always use it. Come up with new ideas for posts. For example, if you have new dishes you're working on, cut them up and bring out samples for the customers. Ask if they would like to try it, and if they like it, ask if you can take a photo and post it. Post about your chef, cook, or staff (if they agree to it), and put a human face to your restaurant. If they volunteer for a cause, ask for a photo to post, such as "Daniel, our server, helps clean up a park for families to enjoy." Look up fun days such as National Spaghetti Day on nationaldaycalendar.com, and promote your restaurant enticing people to "celebrate" a national day with a dish you offer or even create just for the day.

Promote your restaurant, staff, food, and specials, and keep the schedule of postings consistent.

The Second Step

Compile a list of media contacts. Start researching online, and find your local media. How do you do this? Type in "Media List [your state]," and sites listing media outlets will come up.

There is now a second set of people known as *influencers*. These people, while not usually journalists or writers, have created a new outlet with thousands, if not millions, of followers. Celebrities like my friend and favorite food influencer Jonathan Cheban, aka Foodgod, charge tens of thousands of dollars for one mention on social media. You can search social media using terms such as "food" to compile a list of local influencers in your city.

Media people and influencers love being invited in for a comped meal. Now, understand that there is no guarantee they will write, talk, or post about your restaurant. When you invite someone in, you can phrase it as, "I really would like to have you come to my new restaurant to give it a try. If you like it, please write, talk, or post about it and then spread the word. That's all I ask." People will respond yes or no.

One other possibility to promote your restaurant with the media is to hold a private party with invited guests such as the media and influencers. You can hand-pass food or offer a meal during the night. Again, you will have to compile the list to know whom to invite. Personally, I would advise asking the media and influencers personally, or hire a local public relations company to help you host a media night. The media and influencers will show up, but everyone understands that you might have an exceptional chef or staff working to make the evening extra special. That is not a representation of your real restaurant, and if everyone understands your heart and soul as part of this opening, I believe you will get a much better response.

There are many armchair food critics looking for reasons to write bad reviews on social media sites. We addressed this issue in

Chapter 7. As you will find, the professional critics will work with you and give you the chance to succeed. Remember, the professional critics work for a media outlet and really want to write a fair review. But do not take them lightly. If you are consistent and well serviced, you should be fine. A great review will help to drive traffic into your restaurant. Ironically, a mediocre or bad review can also drive traffic into the restaurant in the form of curious diners.

Money Can Buy You Love for Your Restaurant

Advertising is much more than just an ad online, in a magazine, on the radio, or broadcast on television. Advertising is a paid message that tells people who you are, where you are, and what you serve. You need to ensure that your brand is reflected properly. Put thought into what you are conveying, and use the emotion that best fits your brand.

Many sales reps will be knocking on your door to sell you every type of advertising. Let's break it down so you can decide where to budget your money for the biggest bang for your buck and stay on your brand message. You still don't need to make a decision yet about whether you want to hire a marketing or advertising agency to help you navigate. Continue reading.

Getting Specific with Targeted Marketing

One of the things that my company does is IP targeting and retargeting. A *target market* refers to your group of potential customers. This group can be defined in many different ways such as ZIP code, shopping habits, and dining habits, including people who eat at your competitors. We send advertisements directly onto someone's mobile device within applications, articles, and social media. The reader will see a message such as, "Hey, it's 11:30 a.m., you should order pizza for your office today. ABC Pizza is offering a special today for $9.99 that should feed your office." The message ends by 1:00 p.m. Then another message at 4:00 p.m. may say, "Hey, if you order pizza for dinner today, you don't have to cook. ABC Pizza can deliver a hot meal in 30 minutes."

My company recently implemented a nationally targeted marketing campaign for Just LeDoux It Whiskey during the National Finals Rodeo. Chris LeDoux was a famous country and western singer until his passing in 2005. His family served this particular brand of whiskey before he passed away and now distributes Just LeDoux It Whiskey.

We were able to pinpoint people attending rodeo events. First, messages were sent to cell phones and other devices with the Just LeDoux It Whiskey branding. Then we "followed" them home. If a guest lived by a Texas Roadhouse restaurant, which sells Just LeDoux It Whiskey, we targeted them with an ad to come in and have a specialty cocktail.

Such ads don't have to be intrusive. They are on most of the application games people play with their friends. Ads pop up within these apps or in stories people read on their device. This technology is reasonably priced and is something to think about investing in with part of your marketing budget. Think of the checkout lanes in grocery and big box stores filled with candy, mints, and gum. This is impulse buying: while people might not walk into the store thinking they need that stuff, they will pick it up standing in line. Companies that manufacture and distribute candy, mints, and gum pay a lot of money to have their products displayed in those checkout lines. This is the same concept in digital form.

Putting the Web to Work

You should now plan to have your own website. Gone are the days when you needed to spend $5,000 for a website with bells and whistles. With templates and free sites such as WordPress (wordpress .com) and Wix (wix.com), you can make your site easy, simple, and fun. There are lots of templates out there that other restaurants have used, and all you need to do is plug and play different pictures. It's all about images and the menu for customers.

However, your website is really a tool for search engines such as Google, Safari, Bing, and others. You want to be the number-one restaurant in your market when people search for your cuisine. Let's use the example of pizza. I did a search on Google, and the franchise Pizza Hut came up seven times. By the end of the second page, Papa John's finally came up. Pizza Hut pays more money for ads than Papa John's.

Should you pay to get a higher rank on the search sites? Are you using your website properly?

This type of search advertising falls in the programmatic advertising category, which can be either expensive if you hire the wrong team to help or extremely reasonable if you research and hire correctly. I recommend looking into a freelancer website, posting a one-time job description of exactly what you need done, and starting to vet out the applicants.

This person can also be used to create your website if you haven't already developed one or to revise it if necessary to obtain a higher ranking. I suggest budgeting money to hire a freelance person who works with SEO and rankings on browsers. The sites I use to find freelancers are fiverr.com and upwork.com.

Again, you can post on the job order that you need to increase the ranking of your restaurant along with including reviews, menu, phone number, and directions. It should not cost you more than $300. Since you have photos, the best pictures can be displayed.

Banner ads are passé. Today it is ads on phones and devices with a targeted audience. Ads create interaction and follow an algorithm.

Deliver Me from Hunger

One of the most significant and best forms of marketing and advertising in the restaurant business today is delivery services. I highly recommend that you connect with each delivery service available, because they will market your restaurant to every person who uses their services. There are even ghost kitchens: restaurants that are not open to the public and only deliver meals with these services.

I never had that option, and I had to hire my own delivery people. There is my w(h)ine (without cheese and crackers).

It works like this: the higher the percentage you give the service from each order, the better placement you will have on their site. That being said, you should plan to give the delivery services 20% of the bill instead of the usual 10% fee. All of a sudden, you're number one on that delivery site, and they are really promoting you. This is advertising dollars invested very well. According to upserve.com, 60% of the restaurant operators polled stated that offering deliveries through third-party delivery sites had generated bigger food sales. It is also reported that orders placed online will become a $38 billion industry in 2020.

Yes, you have to pay something to be placed number one, but this is marketing, and working with a third-party delivery site has been found to increase sales volume between 10 and 20%. This is something to think about when planning your marketing and advertising budget. By the way, this is money you pay from the order, not up front.

Speaking of Specials

What about coupons through Groupon, Living Social, and other sites that offer specials to a big database of customers?

If you have a concept and you want lots of people to come in the door, they are fantastic. For example, my friend Christina owns a mini-golf business, and she loves Groupon. Her expenses include rent, utilities, and staff. Customers come and pay for two-for-one rounds of golf. If a group of four comes in, there are no additional expenses, and the place gets filled up. The only problem for her is if the course is full and customers are waiting to pay the full price. However, she has an arcade that is not only another revenue center but also lightens up the load on the mini-golf course by keeping customers engaged in other activities.

With a restaurant, it is different. If a customer purchases one of your coupons from the online coupon company, the revenue breakdown is simple: the restaurant receives about 50% of the price paid for the coupon. In essence, the customer will come in with a coupon for 50% off the price of a meal, and you will receive only 25% revenue on that meal. That will eat into your food costs. In my opinion, using those services is not worth it, including the cost to the company. I recommend offering creative specials like half-price steak nights (where you keep 50% of the revenue). This way, you control the loss and gains.

The only benefit is that these coupon websites have enormous databases that reach all their customers and introduce them to your restaurants. That will bring more customers through your door, but at a large cost to you. Just be ready to lose money to gain new patrons.

Do People Still Use Printed Coupons?

Yes, specific demographics do. One of them is an older demographic. However, if you are thinking Boomers, that generation is using apps and can navigate phones and devices. I am speaking about the generation before the Baby Boomers.

There are still companies that offer coupon mailers, and you can target neighborhoods and ZIP codes. Let's say you decide to try a mailer with a 50%-off coupon. A couple comes into the restaurant and orders a meal using the coupon, and you lose the cost of your food by honoring that coupon. Will they return? If they are on a budget, probably not. Factor in the price of sending out the coupons. You are now in the red with this advertising investment, because advertising is an investment.

What about Smaller Publications?

There are small local magazines that target ZIP codes or communities, and newsletters for places of worship. Personally, I would select the house of worship. The ZIP code magazines are great for people looking for a handyman but not so much for a place to eat. Also, you need to run a big ad, not a small quarter-page or business-card-size ad.

According to KruseControlInc.com, in the 1930s (you read that correctly), it was discovered that people needed to hear or see an ad seven times to respond. In today's world, a person needs to see that printed ad many more times than a digital ad (which will get a more immediate response).

Sometimes a sales rep will promise to include an editorial if you buy an ad, meaning an article about your restaurant. It depends on the publication, but most of the time a great editorial write-up works a heck of a lot better than an advertisement. Of course, if any magazine (digital or print) offers to write a story about your restaurant for the cost of a meal, I would say to do it. But unless the publication is one that is distributed around your city, don't buy an ad just to get an article written.

They Are Called the Elite Squad

There is the regular Yelp, and then there is the Yelp Elite Squad. These are reviewers (not critics, writers, journalists, or influencers) who write reviews extensively on Yelp and are invited to join the squad. There are exclusive events for the Yelp Elite Squad, including tastings. Yelp sets up these events, and your restaurant provides the space and food. However, this is *not* media or influencers. These members will write a review based on their opinion, whether it is good or not.

While I understand that reviews are a fact of today's technology, if you choose to participate, you need to give 110%. Bring in the squad, feed them, and get the word out. However, just remember that you are bringing in people with a very critical eye and palate. You can try to mitigate any mistakes or complaints, but this will be a more challenging group to appease. Personally, I am offering better ways to reach out to the community, but I wanted to address Yelpers.

People Who Tour, Stop, Eat, and Go

If your restaurant is in an upscale retail center with other restaurants, you might be approached to participate in a *dine-around*. This is an event to promote the restaurants in the center, where guests stop in each restaurant to taste one dish. If you operate a burger place, you might give out tastings of your fries. There are also food tours where paying guests stop at your restaurant (all scheduled stops) for a tasting, which is usually a course. There are many ticketed foodie events and functions to benefit charity, where booths are set up for guests to sample your food.

I don't know that I've ever heard any restaurateur tell me they've gained more business from these events. Usually they are involved to say hello to their current customers and make that bond stronger, as well as to develop community relations. I've heard plenty of complaints because of the expensive free food being given away with no tangible results. In my experience, if someone's going to complain because they don't believe they got anything out of it, they've already got a bad attitude participating in the event.

Don't do it if you don't want to. If you do want to participate, make sure your greeters are there, with music to fit your image. Project your message in person because this could be the only chance a potential customer will meet you and try your restaurant. Bring your best servers and think about what message you want to project. If it is fun like my hamburger place, project that. If it is a family-style Italian place, showcase that quality. Get business cards, email addresses, post about the event on your social media, and make it enjoyable for you. Your customers know when you are having stress free fun.

If you want to support the charity but don't want to participate with a booth, you can still support the charity by offering a gift certificate for a raffle prize or sending food for the volunteers.

My Head Keeps Spinning

There are spinners, people who stand on busy corners or in front of a business and spin a sign, usually in the shape of an arrow. For some businesses, that is probably an effective way to attract customers. I don't recommend it for restaurants. You would have to incur the costs of making the sign, and there is a fee for someone to spin that sign. There are more effective ways to invest your advertising dollar.

Signs in the Sky

There are also billboards, including electronic billboards, static billboards, and moving billboards. This one is about location, location, location. In Las Vegas, there is a billboard located on the northwest corner of a major one-way street going north. It is strategically placed close to the traffic signal. I have driven this road many times and stared at that billboard while waiting for the light to change. However, there are other billboards located along a thoroughfare with no traffic signals at a speed limit of 45 mph. Have I seen those billboards? Yes, speeding by; and since I don't want to cause an accident, I don't stop to look.

I have seen one effective use of a billboard by a restaurant. This restaurant is located in a strip mall that can easily be overlooked unless you already know the restaurant is located there and are planning to stop in. The owners invested in the billboard at the intersection before the restaurant to let drivers know the restaurant is in the next strip mall. A second billboard has a big arrow pointing down, telling drivers that this is the location of the restaurant. This is very effective, and I am sure people have stopped in because of this advertising.

People Still Watch Television

Yes, people still watch television. However, the days of only three networks or one cable company are long gone. There are cable, satellite, and numerous streaming services. A portion of the population even watches television using an antenna. Just because you buy an ad on a nationally broadcast program, as a local commercial, doesn't mean everyone watching that program will see your ad (which needs to be seen at least seven times to be effective). The commercials you view on cable are different from the ones broadcast on each satellite network and each streaming service. Cable providers offers its own version of a streaming service (watching cable online), even those commercials are different. You would have to buy an ad on each outlet to reach your audience. That is very expensive.

Unfortunately, a trend that's been going on for the last 15 years is pay-for-play TV interview shows. Sometimes, as a restaurant owner, you can get an interview and offer a demonstration for special events such as the Big Game or holidays without paying, because the TV shows want to feature a segment about food. But be prepared for account executives from television stations to come knocking and to offer you an appearance on television for a price. I would wait and provide an interview and demonstration for special holidays instead of paying for it.

Life Is a Trade-off

You have something just as valuable to offer instead of money: you can offer a meal, and most print, broadcast, and digital outlets need a place to bring clients.

Don't go overboard, but offer a trade in exchange for advertising. Select the outlets that will be the most effective for you. In broadcast outlets, tell the account executives that you don't want an ad but to have the on-air talent talk about your restaurant. For print and digital, ask for an article.

Let's say you are giving the outlet a $100 trade and they're going to bring two or three more people in the door. That could be two or three more customers to add to your database, so that makes sense as an advertising investment (and trade is an advertising investment). I did this type of media trading with my floral warehouses. I advertised in trade with a local sports radio program starring former Redskin football player Rick "Doc" Walker and Georgetown University coach John Thompson. When those listeners heard that Rick or John just picked up a dozen roses for only $9.99, there would be customers standing in line out my door. Lucie McKay, who ran the floral warehouses with me, needed a few days to prepare the staff for the mad rush that this type of advertising brought us.

Mention My Restaurant's Name, Please

Let's talk about public relations, which is different from marketing and advertising.

The difference between public relations and advertising is whom you pay. You pay a public relations professional (or firm) to get your message out about your restaurant. In advertising, you pay for the word to get out there, whether you are using an advertising agency, contracting with an outlet, or using other means like sign spinners.

There are public relations firms that specialize in promoting restaurants and food-related events. However, a retainer (set fee) is usually involved, and there are ways you can get the word out without hiring anyone. They will pitch your restaurants to media people to get articles written without you having to pay for an ad. This is called *earned media*. Basically, the media is earned from the relationship between the public relations person and the media outlet.

There are ways you can do that yourself.

My friend Debbie Hall is a publisher, editor, and writer for multiple magazines and digital sites. She has her go-to list of restaurants, restaurateurs, and chefs to get quotes from. If she's writing an article on food safety, food service, or what's trending, she will reach out to these people first. Why? First, she knows them and their reputations. While she does understand that they are working and doesn't expect an immediate response, they acknowledge her messages. If they don't know the answer, they can direct Debbie to the right person. Debbie will pick up the phone, call me, and ask me about some aspect of food and restaurants. I'll give her a quote. The next thing you know, my name's in the publication, and that is great. She will write, "According to Michael Politz, of *Food & Beverage Magazine* . . . ." That is brand recognition. So you get to know Debbie (or someone like her). You invited them in for a meal and offer to give quotes and become a go-to resource. Make it fun, and tag them on social media. Again, this goes back to creating relationships.

The Award Goes To . . .

Let's talk about awards. There are many competitions to enter. Now, for 9 out of 10 awards, you are able to simply purchase the wall plaque, but it still looks cool and is great to post on social media and the walls of your restaurants. So try to enter as many award competitions you can; even if you don't win, it still gets your restaurant name out there.

On a truly legitimate level, you will find that your local community newspapers and magazines probably have best restaurant awards or greatest waiter competitions. On a global scale, you will find Michelin, Top 50, Elite Traveler, James Beard, and Tripadvisor Awards. They each have different entry fees and rules of engagement for entries.

Post that the restaurant is nominated for an award. However, only post a second time if you win the award. If you don't win, don't post anything about that award. Yes, it would be good sportsmanship to post "Congrats to ABC Restaurant for winning the Best Of award," but if your restaurant was nominated for the same award, people are going to wonder why you didn't win. But if you do win, make certain everyone knows.

The Writing's on the Wall

If your restaurant is written up in print, especially a cover story, frame it and hang it up. Hopefully, you will get so many that you run out of wall space. Be sure to take a photo of the article and post it on social media, thanking the writer and publication. That will go a long way in creating a relationship with a member of the press. Also, send your photos with tags to industry publications and social media sites such as *Food & Beverage Magazine*. You can send photos with tags using Facebook Messenger or Direct Message on Instagram, or look up the email address listed on the page.

Don't worry if you don't have a wall of celebrities. In fact, don't ever ask a celebrity who comes into your restaurant to take a picture with you, unless they offer—and it's great if they do. Start a wall with your regular customers, instead. Celebrities don't come back all the time, but the regular customers will return, and they want to be your celebrities. Put their photos up on the wall, thanking them. Post on social media. Sponsor children's or adult sports teams such as bowling or soccer. There are many ways to get your name out there.

Answering the Final Question

Following my advice, hire a public relations firm or social media guru for special projects only, and save a lot of money. As for the advertising agency, there is no need to hire one at the moment.

9 So You Have $25,000 to Spend

As promised, here is the chapter about opening a restaurant for an investment of $25,000. I did it multiple times myself, and now I will share how you can do it, too. You have many yellow pads and documents filled with a lot of information and guidance from reading this book. Now let's put all that to work for you.

It was at a point in my life as a long-time, successful publisher of *Food & Beverage Magazine* that I thought of opening a restaurant with just a small $25,000 investment. I've read enough, I've learned, and I've watched enough failures and witnessed many successes in the hospitality industry. I asked myself, "Why do I want to open a restaurant?"

The Answer Is . . .

I wanted to do what I loved as a kid, and that was hanging out at my favorite restaurant. There was a chain of hamburger restaurants, Little Tavern, on the East Coast in Baltimore, Maryland; Arlington, West Virginia; Washington DC; and surrounding areas. There was one in Georgetown, close to American University (where I attended college), and that became one of our hangouts when I was 18 years old.

My friends and I would go to the Georgetown bars (the drinking age was only 18) and then finish the night at Little Tavern. We would buy a bag of hamburgers stacked with ketchup, mustard, pickle, and onions—simple little sliders on the greatest buns. We always had a great time there. It was very small; I don't even think they had tables. Little Tavern had stools, and most of its business was take-out. In fact, its tagline was "Buy 'em by the bag." For drinks, it was soda or coffee.

I remember watching the cooks in the kitchen with their white outfits, aprons, and paper hats. All of the hamburger meat was mixed with onions and rolled into little balls. Every time someone placed an order, the cooks took out the little balls, slapped them onto the grill, smashed them, and cooked them. They flipped the burgers once and put them on the bun. The meat was always moist. The restaurant used steamer trays to keep the burgers warm, and even at my young age, I could see it was super-old equipment.

The place was always packed when I went there, with a long line at the walkup window. Sadly, the chain went out of business in 2008. I don't know why. But Little Tavern demonstrated a recipe for success with similar restaurants such as White Castle in the Midwest (which has since expanded to 377 locations in 13 states) and Krystal Burgers in the Southeast (with 360 locations in 12 states).

I had an emotional connection to that small hamburger place, and I knew I could create a modern version with the right fries and the right sliders. I knew it would be a success.

My Very First Restaurant

The next question was, "Why didn't I open a restaurant sooner?" The answer is simple: I was scared to lose the money. Finally, the right opportunity came up and I took advantage of it.

Food & Beverage Magazine had become a well-oiled machine with my team of superstars like Bryan Bass (hospitality expert and university professor), Gary Coles (our art director veteran who worked for John Kennedy Jr.'s *George Magazine*), and Max Adler (who became our go-to source), who always got everything accomplished. With this team in place, we were ready to share our experience with the magazine to open a new Las Vegas restaurant.

We had worked a sweetheart deal with an off-Strip property owner, and the property happened to have a fully functioning closed restaurant attached. We partnered with Chef Chris Palmeri, the youngest executive chef in the history of MGM properties, and we were on our way. The name was Hobos and Gypsies, and our target clientele were the hospitality employees of Las Vegas. We literally covered the walls with every influential person we could who worked both on and off the Strip. Bryan and I used all of our vendor relationships to help build our brand. Lots of lessons were learned from that experience, and the biggest lesson was taught to us by the property owner. He had a bigger share of ownership than we did, made very poor marketing and financial decisions, and ultimately closed the restaurant on us—not so much of a sweetheart deal.

My Next Restaurant

I was still determined to open a restaurant, even with the failure of Hobos and Gypsies. I knew I wanted to open a place that served hamburgers, French fries, and shakes. I wanted it to be fun, and I knew that this time I needed at least an equal share if not a bigger share of ownership.

First the Menu, Then the Location

So what's the first thing I did? I grabbed a couple of hospitality industry friends who knew more than I did: Cory McCormick and Phil Shalala. Cory was a management guru, and Phil happens to be one of the greatest marketing minds and brand builders in history. He came up with a famous slogan for a beverage company when they changed their marketing directly to the action sports arena. We already had the recipes, so we began developing a menu first. I met with all my chef friends, and they disagreed on some of the recipes, but I wanted to stick to my concept and moved forward in my own direction. I wanted to re-create those burgers I so enjoyed when I was young.

We looked for places in the classifieds and online, especially Craigslist.com and LoopNet.com. We also reached out to realtors. I would only look at places that already had kitchens with grease traps and hoods. My mistake, which you can avoid, was that while I looked at second- or third-generation restaurant locations with equipment requirements, I didn't research the actual areas.

One of the first places we opened was inside a gas station on a very busy corner. The kitchen had all the equipment, including grills, steam tables, and fryers. The only thing I had to put in there was a soft ice cream machine for milkshakes and a cash register. We found our spot for only $3,500 a month, and we paid the security deposit down and our first month's rent, totaling $7,000. If you are doing the math, that leaves $18,000 in my budget.

What's My Sign?

Next, I knew I needed signage. We negotiated with the landlord to install the sign, and they agreed. I found a graphic artist and gave them the specifications and size of the sign (a signboard with a light from the back). The graphic artist knew another graphics person who could produce the vinyl with the colors I wanted, and everything including installation cost $400 ($17,600 left in the budget).

Show Me the Money

I investigated the different point of sale (POS) systems and various computer systems. Our thought process at this time was with the

intention of scaling larger, which might have been a big mistake.
I didn't need that equipment, just a regular cash register. However,
I did get the POS system. It didn't cost me anything because I
connected it to my credit card merchant services. The merchant
services representative explained their points and percentages, which
were all reasonable. They provided me with a computer with its POS
system at no additional cost to me.

That Red Tape Again

We had the place with an address, we got the licensing, and now it
was time for the health department inspection. Since the department
had already inspected the previous restaurants, they knew its potential
problems, and I could work on correcting them. I am going to repeat
this again: everything has to be spotlessly clean, and you cannot have
any food anywhere during the inspection, or it will compromise the
inspection and the food will be thrown out. The department came
out and approved me. The licensing cost $600 ($17,000 left in
the budget).

My Team

My next step was to hire and train our staff to become team members.
This is where a significant portion of the investment was going to
be spent. Cory made sure the applicants could prepare hamburgers,
French fries, and chili with our special ingredients. We also had to
train everyone on using our system. We then had to figure out who
would work on the schedule, how many employees to hire, and how
much time training would take. Of course, there was the cost of uniforms, and every hour spent in training is an expense.

   While interviewing people, we found out who worked on what
kind of POS systems or cash registers. I asked those applying if they
cooked at a previous job, and what they prepared. We hired people

who previously worked for fast food chains such as Wendy's, Burger King, and McDonald's. These people were used to working in high-volume food production, using a fryer, and preparing hamburgers and French fries. I even hired people who knew how to fix the equipment in case the grill went down, the fryer didn't clean properly, or we had other equipment problems.

We spent about $4,000, and you should plan for $3,000 to $4,000. That estimated $17,000 in the available budget had now decreased to about $13,000.

It Is All About Presentation

We didn't have to go out and buy dishware and tableware since we used plastic utensils and Styrofoam containers. However, I had to buy a lot of napkins and cups. Still, that was the good news since the gas station took care of the other paper supplies for the community bathroom.

However, let's talk about using Styrofoam ware. What are you putting into the Styrofoam container? We were putting in hamburgers and fries, and they "sweat." This means steam drips from the top of inside the lid down onto the buns. I had to make certain to have holes so my Styrofoam containers were vented. You'll start noticing lots of minutiae. As you're slowly opening your restaurant, you can make changes without buying too much stuff in the beginning.

Where Should I Buy My Food?

Now came the time to buy and stock the food. I thought that was going to be the easy stuff. I had already spoken to the vendors and thought I knew what to have on hand.

I knew we needed packets of ketchup, mustard, and mayonnaise.

But how much food would I need, including spices and seasonings? All of a sudden it was scary, because I didn't want to run out of food.

I knew the condiments would not go bad, but what if we went through the supplies too fast?

I had to figure out how many pounds of hamburger and how many buns we needed. This was scary because they were perishable and could go bad, costing us money. I had to make a decision and see what sold and almost have the perishable items run out. I also knew where to go to pick up more supplies at a moment's notice.

Smart and Final and Restaurant Depot are good places to have close to you because you (or a staff person) can go get more supplies. This is how I discovered why you don't want to get too much into specialized products. I used vinegar powder as one of my ingredients and couldn't source it locally. I had to purchase it online and have it shipped. Then I ran out of vinegar powder and luckily found an Asian supermarket that happened to have something similar that worked in the recipe. I also used dehydrated onions, and we ordered that ingredient in bulk. I used so much of it, and it was such an essential ingredient in our hamburgers, that we could not run out.

Let's talk about buns. You don't want to have a large supply of hamburgers and run out of buns. This is not the time to run to the supermarket and find something comparable. Customers will notice immediately it's a different bun than the one you purchase from your restaurant supplier. They will tell you and also tell others.

We were picky about pickles. I had to get the #10 can of Heinz dill pickles (that brand specifically). It is a little dill pickle slice, and it's probably been packed in that water for 10 years. The vendors from Sysco and US Foods tried to get me to buy their fresh dill pickles. I didn't want the fresh dill pickles because they were a completely different flavor. I had to buy cases and cases of cans of these pickles, so we never ran out.

I didn't use tomato, fresh onion, or lettuce on my burgers. They were just straight-up sliders. Of course, we used a particular brand of American cheese, understanding that each cheese melts differently, and we had to be consistent. I had to be careful with cheese because sometimes we couldn't get the slices apart—the cheese had been frozen, then defrosted, and then frozen again.

Buying the food was another $6,000 in expenses. That available budget had now shrunk to $7,000.

Enjoy a Birthday Cake All Year 'Round

I decided to sell slices of birthday cake for dessert. Oh my God, it was kitschy and a great marketing pitch. Believe it or not, I couldn't find a supplier of a simple birthday cake among my restaurant suppliers. I had to consider buying the cake from Costco and cutting it up into pieces, but at a very high cost per piece, made it too expensive. I wouldn't be able to mark up the price on the cake to make any profit.

I finally found a local wholesale bakery that would bake and decorate birthday cakes for us at less than $1 per piece. We eventually started purchasing our burger buns from them as well. The buns ended up being about the same cost they were from the food distributor, but I wanted to build goodwill with the bakery by giving them more business. I also had to prepare for Sundays and holidays when they were closed; what if we needed more buns because we sold out of our inventory?

The Main Entrée

The specialty item of the restaurant was the burgers.

While working on the recipe and cooking them the same every time, the first problem was using prepackaged burgers; every time we took out a package of pre-frozen burgers, they were packaged stacked like dominos. We had to chisel each piece off, because for some reason they had defrosted and then refrozen. We couldn't get the meat out fast enough. Then we started using fresh meat and adding dehydrated onions. We finally learned to rehydrate the onions in water first. On the next attempt, we mixed a specific portion into the meat and made one-ounce patties. After finding that right balance, we took the mixture and rolled it into balls. I wanted my cooks to slap them down, smash them, cook them, and put them in the buns.

The problem was the time from the order to cooking them—there was not enough time. There were lines out the door. I learned that we had to make the burgers in advance and put them in steamer tables, using the correct tops to allow airflow without making the buns soggy. Thank you, restaurateur Carlos Silva, for that piece of advice. We kept that recipe and finally knew how to make the burgers in less time.

What Would You Like to Drink?

What kind of soda do you want to sell? You can sell by the can, bottle, soda gun, or self-serve soda machine. What brand of soda? Will you sell bottled water or offer complimentary glasses of water (from the tap)?

We sold a particular brand of soda in cans, and I found that if I purchased cases of that soda from Restaurant Depot rather than directly from the soda supplier, the cost was 20% less. That means I made 20% more per can of soda I sold. I wrote down the costs and bought wherever I could save money—every dollar matters.

Build It, but Will Customers Come?

My place was open, and now I needed to get customers.

We used digital media, especially Facebook. We created a page and then created a plan for our Facebook ads. I targeted people with the algorithm who loved White Castle or Krystal Burgers, and our ads popped up when they were on Facebook.

People who loved French fries were targeted. I posted pictures of French fries, and the tagline was "Fries before guys." I created the ad in pink to target women of all ages.

I created a cute logo with a little character mascot, and we always included the logo in our posts. We took pictures of the little burgers, soda, and fries as a special for $4.99. I made sure the photos showed little burgers, so customers knew these were not regular-sized burgers. We had lines out the door because we targeted the right people. We also ran a Facebook promotion in which the person who tagged the most people about our restaurant won a free meal. So we had hundreds of people being tagged, bringing more awareness to our restaurant.

We tried to choose some great price points, and we knew we should sell burgers in multiples. We came up with funny names to encourage customers to buy the case or a big meal with 24 sliders, 4 drinks, and 4 French fries for $30. People bought them in mass quantities.

With the digital age, you can create a budget of $10 per day to place ads on social media. If you are technically challenged, visit freelance.com or Upwork.com and search for social media ad freelancers online. In your job order, you need to write that you are looking for someone to place advertising on your social media or digital media in specific areas (popup ads on apps, for example), and you only have $30. People will negotiate and tell you they can do it for $20. They can create the ads for you. They can run your digital advertising campaign through all of your social media. They can perform demographic targeting and granulation. The cost, including advertising, will probably be around $100.

My Failure Became My Success

There were long lines and longer waiting times, and that problem became my failure. We got overwhelmed because of all the marketing we were doing on social media. We had lines out the door, and the cooks couldn't keep up. It wasn't a matter of the kitchen not being big enough or not having enough supplies. The cooks couldn't make the product fast enough, and people complained. Our customers loved our food, but they complained about the wait, and that was a failure on my part.

I stood back there, sweating, yelling at the cooks, and trying to run my magazine at the same time, knowing that this was just about to implode on us. Customers were waiting and complaining, and I gave away free food. I learned from my mistakes and turned it around by scaling differently.

I Expanded My Menu

As you're making money, slowly introduce new products that complement the menu and build up your clientele, because people want something different. At the hamburger places, we eventually added a chicken sandwich. I made my own dressing, and the secret formula was mixing buttermilk ranch dressing with curry powder. People lost their minds, they loved it so much.

I had no idea why everyone loved the recipe, but all I did was order the cheapest buttermilk ranch dressing in the big tub. I added curry powder, mixed it up, and created a magic sauce. I could have bought a fine, high-end brand of dressing. I didn't need to do that, and neither do you. Make your own fry sauce using inexpensive ketchup and mayonnaise, and it will taste delicious. Maybe add some sugar or bacon, because everything tastes better with sugar and bacon.

Considering Other Types of Restaurants

When you are opening a restaurant for $25,000, it's mainly casual dining. But you can still go bigger and open a restaurant for about $25,000.

But I Want to Open a Sit-Down Restaurant

If you're opening a sit-down restaurant, depending on the size, you're going to need to buy more food. Can you mitigate those costs? Of course you can. If you want to open a bigger establishment with the right budgeting and research, you can do it.

Remember, just because you have more seats doesn't mean you need a bigger kitchen staff. You may need more bus people or more servers. The same digital strategy campaigns can be used to bring in customers. Coupon sites like Groupon and LivingSocial can also help drive awareness of your restaurant and bring in new customers.

Be prepared to lose 50% with these coupon services, which will eat into your food costs. I used Groupon with a special of 10 burgers for $8. People bought the coupon and used it, and I only made $4 per coupon. I lost money on that deal, but it brought people in; and I only ran the special for a very short period of time, mitigating any chance for a devastating loss.

All You Need Is a Kitchen

I am in love with the concept of ghost kitchens, where all you do is rent the kitchen. You only need to hire a cook. My friend Jason Manly has always been an innovative restaurateur and created a cheesesteak concept. He goes into a ghost kitchen from 11:00 a.m. to 4:00 p.m. to cook his cheesesteaks. He only accepts delivery orders, so customers order, and the food is delivered to them using a third-party delivery service. Jason sells up to 50 cheesesteaks a day and is making money from it because his expenses are so low. It's a brilliant concept.

However, I know it's not as fun and not as personally engaging as opening a restaurant. You don't get to engage with your customers, and you rarely get immediate feedback. But Jason is making money cooking, and you can as well. If you have a product such as pizza, cookies, or sandwiches that can be easily delivered, this is a great concept to consider.

Opening a Steak House on a Shoestring Budget

You can open a steak house for about $30,000. Now, what kind of steak house can you open for that kind of money? You're not going to be able to open a world-famous Peter Luger Steakhouse or The Palm, because you won't have the money to invest in the decor alone. But think of this as plug and play. If you find a space that comes fully equipped with everything you need, including tables and chairs, you can make it happen.

You go through the same process mentally. You've got to come up with a menu that doesn't offer 50 different kinds of steak, because the meat is expensive. However, I recently spoke to someone who had a concept for a steak house where marinated steak was sold at $2 per ounce. The meal included potatoes, salad, and soup. They made extra income on the desserts that they displayed on carts. The restaurateur loved to sell cobblers for dessert because the profit margin was extremely high.

You can open a restaurant that is that simple with a good recipe for steak that is delicious. If the restaurant is successful, you can offer specials during the week or at different times. But if you have one item that comes with a potato, salad, and soup, you can control your costs. You bake the potatoes, salad is premade, the soup comes in a bag, and a cook prepares the steak one way. You can offer a video camera at the weigh station where the meat is cut, and customers can see how much steak they are getting. The only equipment you would need is a simple iPad—or be creative and use a baby monitor!

$25,000

This is how I opened a restaurant for $25,000. It was blood, sweat, and tears, because we were mopping our own floors and cleaning our own pans. But I learned that the key is to watch your food costs and labor costs. If you can keep those two things down, you can do it.

There will be miscellaneous expenses, and there is marketing. When I opened the restaurant, I had about $6,000 left in the budget. I recommend that you allocate about $500 toward your marketing efforts, as discussed in Chapter 8.

By following my advice in this book, you can also open a restaurant for $25,000. You need to take one more step, and that is in the next chapter.

10 Persevering Through the Tough Times

The one thing I cannot stress enough to you is, *do not fear the failure.* Your internal drive has led you to this point. Try new ideas and concepts using the skills outlined in this book. Some will work and many will fail, but that is all part of the process to succeed. I have taught you everything I can at this point for your success.

Remember this: go with your gut. Follow your instinct. Don't listen to negativity. Hear it, but don't listen to every single thing people say. Always be ready, willing, and able to test new ideas, marketing campaigns, menus, items, staff, and software. Another major thing you can't do is take anything personally.

Develop a Thick Skin

Your restaurant is your dream, and you've poured your heart and soul (and savings) into it. And as hard as it is to do, you *cannot* take anything personally. Your restaurant is about your food and customers, not about you (though it may not feel that way). In the course of a day, you'll hear the following comments and more:

- The French fries were soggy.
- The French fries are too crispy.
- The French fries are amazing.
- The buns are too hard.
- The buns are too soft.
- The buns are delicious.
- Your steak is too tender.
- Your steak is too tough to cut.
- This is not a steak cooked rare.
- Your steak is like butter.

My personal favorite is when someone asks, "Why does the soda taste funny?" You can open a can of soda, pour it into a glass, and bring it to someone, and they will still ask, "Why does the soda taste so funny? Is there something wrong with your gun?" You know you just poured it out of the can. Why would it taste funny?

So expect this, expect the worst, and love the best. If you can be ready for the negativity, imagine how you're going to be for the positivity. I just want to make sure you never take it personally. Don't ever assume anything. If someone's making a face, you could freak out and think they do not like something. They could love your food and just be reacting to a conversation about something that has nothing to do with the food.

Don't assume, and don't take things personally. You will then succeed in being positive. I try to keep a clear mind, and I think if you can keep a clear mind, you can get through any problems. Those thoughts are like seeds that grow and will throw you off your game and make you question your abilities. That being said, we also need to look at the concept of failure.

If You Try Anything, There Will Be Failures

There are going to be failures, bad days, and great days. You'll have horrible days where you will make no money and fantastic days with a big profit. Take it all with a grain of salt. Look at the big picture in the end. It's enjoyable to get excited, high-five staff, share social media posts about your successes, and celebrate. Of course, you want to do that. Then comes a down-in-the-dumps day, but that is still cool. Just keep going with the flow and move on. Remember that slow and steady wins the race.

I cannot stress enough for you not to panic. Think of your business like water flowing from a spigot; if you grab at the water, you will get not any, and that is what will panic you. However, if you slowly cup your hand, you will fill your hand and can drink forever.

Did I Just Hear an Excuse?

If it is a bad day, a bad week, or a bad month, don't come up with excuses.

If there is road work and the street is torn up from construction, making traffic horrible, that is not the reason people are not coming into your restaurant.

Maybe you lease space as a third-generation restaurant, and it remains empty. I know of many spaces that have been leased as several restaurants, only for each restaurant to close in a short period of time. It's not cursed. You don't need to sage the place.

The temperatures are scorching or freezing cold, and people are not coming to your restaurant. If this was the reason, why do people go to other restaurants in the pouring rain or bad weather?

You tell people that Millennials don't like the dishes you are offering, or Boomers eat a different kind of food than what is on your menu.

It is an excuse if you blame the location, the weather, or any other factors at this point.

What you need to do is figure out why people aren't coming into your restaurant. Who cares why they didn't go to the restaurant that was there previously? There's a reason that restaurant failed. You have a different reason why you are not getting customers, and you need to figure that out. If you say it's your location, then close this book and find another business.

Customers will come to the restaurant if your service is excellent and your food is wonderful. Yes, consider all the circumstances, but don't make excuses. If there is a problem, fix it. If there is a challenge, overcome it. This is *your* dream, and while I can share advice, knowledge, and expertise, it is up to you to make it happen.

The Golden Rule

I can't say this enough: be of service, especially to your staff. The last thing you need is an employee telling everyone how badly you run your restaurant. You don't need staff members bickering with each other. This bitterness will implode, especially in tight quarters like a kitchen or a small restaurant environment. This could involve your customers as well, and you don't want that. You just want to be of service. Everybody's equal. You're as equal as the cook and dishwasher. If you're too good to wash dishes, mop your floors, and take out the garbage, close this book and pick another one off the shelf, because this is not the business for you.

Are You Dreaming of Expanding?

If you have done all these great things, if you are of service to everybody, and if your food is excellent, you will make money. Now that you're making money, you're thinking to yourself—and, of course, your friends are telling you—that you need to open a restaurant on a different side of town. People will ask you if you have ever considered opening one in Los Angeles; Rutherford, New Jersey; Potomac, Maryland; or wherever. This is called *scaling up*. Do you want to scale up? And, more importantly, are you ready to scale up? Are you prepared to make a chain out of your locations?

Scaling up is not as simple as it sounds. Restaurant owner(s) who have scaled up and failed do so for many reasons. They were not of service to everybody. They did not go with their gut. They didn't mitigate the cost of labor. There are many factors to success and failure.

If you have your systems in place in your first restaurant, you must have everything in writing (literally). I don't care how simple or minuscule; it's *A* to *Z*. This is how you turn off the light: lift your finger, go to the light switch, and push the light switch down (or flick it down, or grab it with two hands or two fingers and push it down). If you're going to scale, this is how you have to do it. It is a laborious process because you can't be split into two, three, four, or five people. If you can't find someone as vested as you in the business, don't do it. I have seen many restaurants that have tried to open other locations go down the drain. The concept was good, the food was fantastic, and the staff were great. But there was not another person with the same heart, soul, and vested interest as the owner who opened the first location, so both locations failed.

Other people will urge you to franchise your restaurant, which is different from opening a chain (where you maintain total ownership and responsibility). There are different levels to franchising, from opening a restaurant that duplicates the original to just licensing the concept. Are you prepared for it to fail? Because that failure will lead right back to your original location.

It Is Not About Duplication

You got practical advice about opening a restaurant, it is becoming successful, and you think to yourself, I'm going to duplicate that business. Everyone will follow what I did exactly, and the new restaurant will also be successful.

I've tried it, I've done it, and it doesn't work. I sold four of the hamburger places that I had opened (each of them) for $25,000. The new owner couldn't duplicate what we were doing. As I mentioned earlier in the book, he added chicken wings and nachos; in the end, it wasn't the same place. The name of the brand was the same, but everything else was different because there was so much going on instead of our concept, which was simple. He was struggling and trying to fight for success, but he wasn't following the basic principles. There were too many locations, and he didn't have someone at each location to properly follow the rules of engagement for his brand. So the restaurants eventually failed for him.

I did this with the flower shops, too. I thought that I could open a successful flower shop in locations where previous flower shops had failed. I was wrong. I failed hard, costing me hundreds of thousands of dollars. Luckily, I was in my early 20s, so I had another 60 years to worry about my future. I learned that lesson, and now I am sharing it with you.

You may not have that option. Are you in a position that you can open several restaurants at the same time and have them fail big? Maybe you should stick to one place, especially if you are doing fantastic business.

Questions to Ask If You Still Have the Dream of Expanding

If you have your heart set on expanding, ask yourself these questions: Do I scale up? Do I make this a chain? What do I do? How do I keep everything the same? How do I follow those rules of engagement and run each place the same way with the same principles?

You think to yourself that lots of people love your place. My advice is, don't do it. Don't scale up. It's a scary thing. Even with a husband and wife team, I still don't think it's a good idea. I don't see any positives in multiple units, and I think you're going to end up taking money from the first success to pay for the failures of the second.

The Space Next Door Just Opened Up

Now let's talk about scaling up just the one place.

First, here is an example of what can happen. There used to be a great little bar called Huey's on Maryland Parkway in Las Vegas. The place was known for its peanut butter cocktail, and it was just a fun place to hang out. People loved it, and business was thriving. Then the owner decided to upscale his place. He moved the restaurant to a free-standing building a couple of miles from his original location. He changed it totally to include a party room and fine dining, and, of course, he increased prices. It went out of business in a short period of time.

Now let's consider your current location. Let's say it is a fantastic Italian restaurant, and the space next door opens up and is available for lease. You believe that if you lease it and put in 20 more tables, that will equal more revenue. The next question should be, can your kitchen (staff and food inventory) handle that extra business? What is in that space? Do you need another kitchen? But the most critical question is, do you have a line out your door? Because if you don't have a line out your door, you don't need more tables.

I can almost hear you now: "But this is such a great opportunity. I can open a banquet room. I can do weddings and private parties, and I can cater. I can bring in a lot of money and revenue."

My next question is how many people have asked you about a banquet room. Then I have other questions, such as "How much is the rent?" If the rent is $2,000 for the space, you're going to have to fix it up. I would estimate that you will have to invest at least $5,000 for the upgrade. You may have to upgrade to a new sound system, because you can't offer an event space without a good sound system. You may need more audio and visual equipment along with televisions. You're going to need a stage and a dance floor. That goes well above $5,000. You may even need new bathrooms. Go back to your research, and start to look at this as a new business. Do the numbers work? Is it needed in the area? Are customers asking for it?

Unless you have worked in the event business, I recommend that it is probably not the best idea to commit to that extra space as a banquet hall. It's going to take your time and money away from your current source of income: the restaurant. It won't benefit you, because you're not going to do it with a 100% effort. If you don't do it with 100% of your energy, people won't want to pay the 100% pricing. So you'll have to offer less expensive food, and that's not representative of the food you're selling in your restaurant.

You're going to lose money in your restaurant, and this banquet room can be an unnecessary drain. I advise you not to scale up and not to lease the space next door. I've seen too many restaurants expand their space, move to bigger locations, and ruin everything they have achieved.

If There Are Problems, Don't Close, Scale Down

Let's talk about scaling down. What if things aren't working right now? What can you do if you feel like you're hemorrhaging money? What if the business is not performing the way you anticipated?

You have to scale back the staff first, without reducing your service. Maybe you don't have someone standing at the front seating people. You can now have the policy that when a server is open, they go onto the front and seat guests at a table. Do you have family members who can work for no salary? You can clean the place yourself, so you don't have to pay someone to clean.

However, don't reduce your staff and then reduce the quality of the work, food, or service, because customers will notice. If 10% of your income comes from the lunch crowd, close for lunch and save the money, food costs, and overhead. You can change the hours again to open longer hours if there is a demand.

However, you can make those hours count and work your way up. Use the time as prep time. Sometimes you may get a delivery order or big office lunch order that you didn't expect to have that day. But if you're closed, you're not going to get it. Let's talk about multi-job purposes for individuals. Take a hard look at that. Are you offering delivery? Work on these services, because it's free marketing. Consider adding delivery services, and don't get in your own way with your ego.

When the restaurant is closed, you can rent the space for networking groups, meetings, and private parties. This option offers lots of extra income. For example, Lawry's The Prime Rib is, in my opinion, the most delicious prime rib place in the country. They are not open for lunch. But they offer the space for meetings and other events. Lawry's makes sure the food that is served at these meetings and luncheons is the same food served at dinner. Use this exact model.

People are tasting your food at these events, so consider it a taste test. If they like your food, they will come in for dinner. Charge for it, but go over, above, and beyond. If you found a location in an office park, and business dies down after 5:00, don't sell dinner. But you can cater and use those hours for networking groups and private parties. Come up with some really creative marketing ideas for additional revenue.

Why Is This Happening to Me?

Next, you need to figure out your problems and why you're not making money.

Go through your checklist. Why am I not making money? Is it my service? Is it my attitude? Is it my food? Is it my hours? Is it my staff?

Scale back momentarily with the intention of going back to what you were doing, but figure out what you're not doing.

When scaling back, you may want to make drastic changes like changing your ingredients. This is not an option. For example, you might be using fresh, very expensive high-end cheese, and you want to switch and use a more inexpensive cheese to save costs. Guess what? It's too late for that, and you've chosen to use this cheese. If you start switching ingredients and people notice, those people will not come back. Now you have compounded your problem. Talk to your vendors, and ask for better prices. If you can't negotiate lower costs for the food items you use, start looking at trends for potential menu changes to less costly ingredients. If you have to change your food, I would add menu items using food that costs less. If it fits with your cuisine, add something like French fries or mashed potatoes. You can cut back *slightly* on the portion of meat or other expensive items served (without changing the ingredients), add the potatoes (at a lower cost to you), and still serve a full meal at a great value while reducing some food expenses.

So what you need to do is scale down a little bit. Learn how to save money. You're bringing in money; you also need to bring more customers in the door.

Are you upselling items such as appetizers, drinks, and desserts? Start thinking of ways to upsell. If your food is on par as we talked about, you know what people want; they'll spend an extra eight bucks on a piece of cake. Customers are going to want it. I don't care how stuffed they are; people love dessert. Don't feel that you are "taking" money from people; you are offering other choices, and people will say yes or no.

The only thing you can't change is your location, but you certainly can improve your marketing. There are ways to do it, and you need to really investigate what you can do internally and externally to rebuild that business.

It Really Is a Roller Coaster Ride

If you are on a roller coaster, you see things first going up a hill, and then all of sudden you are going downhill. Don't panic if you have to scale back. But don't step on the brakes. You need to keep the momentum to go back up another hill. I am going to repeat— do not slam on the brakes. Change the way you're doing it; keep the momentum. You know you're going down a hill, so scale it back a little.

Keep the restaurant going. But don't let your staff or customers see you sweat. Don't whine and tell everyone that you're not making any money. Tell your team you're just changing their hours, or figure out a way to make it work. But you have to keep that momentum going, and you can zip right back up. So it's not a matter of closing your doors. If you did everything right, there's a problem. Figure out what that problem is, or go back and reread the book. Maybe something else will click, and you'll realize what mistake you might've made, and you can change it.

It is your business, your dream, and your life, so stick to it. Your determination and fortitude are what will work to make your business a success.

FINAL THOUGHTS

Now that you have read the book, I hope I have helped you learn about opening a restaurant through my experiences, knowledge, and advice.

When I first launched *Food & Beverage Magazine* over 20 years ago, my goal was simple. I wanted to ensure that in every issue, somebody would learn something or be inspired in some way. I wanted my readers to discover something within themselves to become an entrepreneur or restaurateur. I wanted to help them gain exclusive success with my magazine. I wanted the articles to inspire ingenuity, excitement, and creativity. I wanted to create something that would ignite a spark in someone from something that they read. The magazine showcased other people's successes and how they were doing it in the hospitality industry, and I wanted others to realize that they can accomplish this, too.

This is the first time I have written a book, and I am hoping my experiences spark the desire inside you to follow your dreams and open a restaurant. Because you are reading this book, I know you were probably exploring becoming an entrepreneur or a restaurateur. You may already be a restaurateur and just need a little help, motivation, and guidance. Whatever your reason for picking up and reading this book, I want to inspire, educate, and inform you.

Would I Like to Write a Book?

I was approached about writing a book from my perspective on how to open a restaurant for $25,000, and I was thrilled beyond words.

During this process, I have learned a great deal as I put my thoughts and experiences into these written words.

I know a big part of my education was publishing *Food & Beverage Magazine* for all those years, filled with articles about successes in the hospitality industry. I learned from being in kitchens with great chefs as well as discussing public relations professionals' pitches for story ideas. All the places I have been and all the things I've experienced have enabled me to write this book. As the process of writing this book became real, it became very challenging to make sure I gave you, the reader, the right information that will help in your inspiration. In the end, I want you to have too much information, if there is such a thing.

I talked about writing your list on your yellow legal pads (or device). I talked about research and doing more research. Think of it as putting everything you discover as well as all the information and resources into one basket. When trouble lurks, you can go into that "basket" and pick out which tool you need to succeed. You will be able to be calm and not intimidated by issues. The information and resources you need are all right here for you. If, for some reason, that tool is not what you need, you know it is okay to go back and do more research, because your answer is out there. Write it out, and hopefully think about it in a way that's clear and precise, instead of having someone try to sell you something and tell you the advantages. You now have the knowledge to say, "Wow, this tool will work for me!" or "This tool will not work for me." Always go with your gut!

Now It is Up to You

You have read the book, and I hope your restaurant is open and you are finding great success and satisfaction. The restaurant should be not a job, but your life's passion. Yes, family, friends, and other aspects of your life should be just as important; but for those who cannot even imagine living their life without opening a restaurant, regardless of where you are in life, I raise a glass and toast you.

Cheers; and, in the unparalleled famous words of my mentor Robin Leach, I wish you "champagne wishes and caviar dreams."

ACKNOWLEDGMENTS

I want to thank my parents for all the life lessons they taught me. As much as I might've kicked and screamed all along the way, I did learn a lot of lessons about being a self-starter and staying motivated, especially from my father. Dr. Murray Politz was thought of not as an entrepreneur, but as a podiatric surgeon. However, I believe he truly was an entrepreneur, and medicine was his tool and his craft. The practice that he built grew because of his marketing abilities. He acquired great medical expertise, but it was because of his drive and ingenuity as an entrepreneur that he built such a fantastic practice and was able to retire at 53 years old.

I learned from him that it is about being of service. Whether you're talking about a patient in a doctor's office or a customer in a restaurant, it is all about being of service with a smile. My mother, Betty (Cookie) Politz, was a registered nurse, and they started the practice together. Patients would travel to see my parents in the office and chat with them about their family and ours. When I was younger, not a day went by that I didn't come across a patient who told me how they loved my mother's smile or that they used to see me in the office as a baby and how my father fixed their feet. That is the true testament of a great businessman.

I had many friends in the restaurant business, and they became great mentors. Neil Segal and his sons Devon and Noel had a significant equipment distribution business in the Washington, D.C. area. I learned a lot from them about the industry. That was probably the prime reason I started *Food & Beverage Magazine*, because they showed me how there was an underserved target market for hospitality information.

When I first started publishing the magazine, it was with great fortune that I met a television icon who was vital to the food and beverage industry and helped launch the Food Network. His name was Robin Leach, of the iconic television series *Lifestyles of the Rich and Famous*. He truly took me under his wing and navigated me through the hospitality world. He filled me with all the knowledge of publishing that he learned from working with media powerhouse Rupert Murdoch. He did it with open arms, opening doors, and no ego involved.

One of the many great things Robin did to open doors was to introduce me to Chef Wolfgang Puck. Wolfgang handed me a huge binder of all of his vendors and told me to reach out to them and tell them that he was my friend and together we were building my magazine. It was a very kind thing for him to do. This is one way I grew my magazine with inside information and valuable insights into the food and beverage industry.

Robin also introduced me to the great restaurateur Piero Selvaggio. Among his numerous awards for his many restaurants, Valentino was named the Best Italian Restaurant in America. There were times when I would speak at early morning lectures at trade shows, and to my surprise, I would look up, and Piero would be sitting in the back row of the room, showing me his support. At the time, I was green and didn't know what I was doing, so I faked it until I made it. There he was, sitting in a room at 7:30 a.m. Piero had gotten up early just to watch me speak and support me. Those are the things that really demonstrate the kindness and support of the hospitality industry.

My gratitude goes to the James Beard–honored innovator and matriarch, Elizabeth Blau. Of all the gifts, lessons, and memories Elizabeth has given to me, none is more precious than introducing me to my best friend, my brother Chef Kerry Simon, whom we lost all too soon to the devastating disease MSA.

I met Kerry when he and Elizabeth, one of the world's most respected restauranteurs and leaders in our industry, opened their restaurant at Peter Morton's Hard Rock Hotel and Casino in Las Vegas. I met Kerry because of Elizabeth's personal invitation to the opening night of Simon's Kitchen and Bar. Our bond was immediate and eternal. Kerry and I spoke nearly every day. The expression, "May his memory be for a blessing is the narrative of my life," fits very well. Every day I remember Kerry, my brother, and every day I am blessed. This book is an expression of my limitless memories of Kerry. Thank you to Elizabeth for doing that introduction for me and making me a part of Kerry's life and allowing me to learn and grow. I've met a lot of wonderful people through her friendship, and along with Kerry, I built some beautiful lifelong relationships.

The unending support of friends such as restaurateur Gary Canter of the legendary Canter's Deli in Los Angeles and rockers Kevin DuBrow of Quiet Riot and Vince Neil of Motley Crue has added a great deal to my life. All have gone above and beyond to make sure *Food & Beverage Magazine* is at the forefront of everything they do in the industry.

Legendary boxer Mike Tyson and his wife Lakiha are my dearest friends. There have been many occasions when Mike and his wife have opened doors for me and introduced me to very high-profile people, kindly telling them that I am an important person to know in the restaurant business. There have been occasions when we dined at restaurants together, and the chefs have sent out multiple specialty dishes. Mike likes to selflessly tell me that we are getting special treatment because I am so important to the industry, while I am honored that he says this. I think we all know that the chefs are sending out the food to impress him. His friendship and influence have helped me in ways I can't begin to list.

Three special friends, Michele Tell, Debbie Hall, and Jennifer English, have been instrumental in writing this book. Without them, I wouldn't have been able to really pinpoint and dial in on the whys and whats of all I have learned and then been able to express the concepts properly. I met both Michele and Debbie at the Las Vegas launch party of *Food & Beverage Magazine* in 2001. Michele is the owner of an award-winning PR agency that pushes the PR envelope: Preferred Public Relations. Debbie is an editor, writer, broadcaster, and foodie who has lived in Las Vegas since 1978. Jennifer is a James Beard award-winning journalist and a powerhouse in the food and beverage world. Jennifer and Debbie both helped push me to the max of my knowledge for the book, sharing their knowledge and expertise about different aspects of the food and beverage industry.

I would additionally like to recognize the family and friends who have helped to support and inspire my entrepreneurial spirit: my sister Dr. Jodi Politz and brother Brian Politz, my uncles Eugene Sandler and Herbert Kaufman, my aunts June Mandel, Natalie Sandler, and Gerry Kaufman, and my cousins Stephan Kaufman, Rene Sandler Esq., Mark Sandler, and Mark Mandel.

I want to thank my friends who have listened to my crazy business ideas for too many years to count: Kenny Rose, Ricky Fangonil, Julian Radice, Lucie McKay, David Sims, Brett Orlove, Collin Millington, Terry Hart, Bryan Bass, Liza Taarud, Mason Martinez, Gary Coles, and Randi Ploff.

I need to thank Alec Shankman and Simon Green from Abrams Artists. Thanks also for the expert help and guidance of my Wiley publishing team including Brian Neill and Vicki Adang. I also want to thank Jon Lovitz, Janie Hoffman, Michael Godard, Wyland, Steve Kaufman, Jon Orlando, Kai, Fiji, and Damon Elliott for always helping me understand my artistic and creative flows.

ABOUT THE AUTHOR

Michael Politz embraced the entrepreneurial spirit as a child, along with a love for the hospitality industry. His first work experience in the food service industry was as a busboy at a white-tablecloth restaurant at the age of 14. As a teenager, Politz operated an ice cream truck business and developed it into an enterprise of frozen food distribution to a retail consumer base. Politz then moved into the floral distribution market as the founder of American Wholesale Floral, an international multi-unit chain of wholesale distributorships of fresh flowers and floral products, and was named to *Entrepreneur* magazine's prestigious Top 40 Under 40. He also graduated with a BSBA from American University, where he served as an adjunct professor in business in the Kogod School of Business.

Politz started *Food & Beverage Magazine* on the East Coast as the go-to resource and food and beverage industry leader. He branched out to the West Coast, settling in Las Vegas as his base during the restaurant boom in southern Nevada. *Food & Beverage Magazine* now boasts over 12 million monthly readers.

He then craved the hamburgers of his youth from his favorite restaurant and decided to re-create that experience by opening Quickee Burgers. Politz chose to take on the challenge of opening a restaurant for $25,000, which he replicated with four burger places that he eventually sold.

Politz has consulted for many Fortune 500 companies, has placed chefs in hundreds of restaurants, and has established several high-profile casino projects. He was involved in the development of projects such as multi-million-dollar licensing deals at The Hard Rock Hotel and Casino and SLS Las Vegas, including entertainment deals. He also helped to conceptualize the highly successful Sugar Factory chain. Politz is one of the four founding brand team members of Ciroc Vodka and has launched many other spirits and wine brands to success.

Politz lives in Las Vegas with Kaiulani and their blended family Shelby, Julien, Amora, and Jett and continues to seek new opportunities as well as share his knowledge and expertise in the hospitality industry that he loves so much.

INDEX